THE CITIZEN'S GUIDE TO
FIFTH GENERATION WARFARE

How To Fight Artifical Intelligence (AI)
Session 2

Michael T. Flynn, LTG, U.S. Army, (Retired)
Boone Cutler, SGT, U.S. Army, (Retired)

The opinion of 10,000 men is of no value
if none of them know anything about the subject.

Marcus Aurelius | Roman Emperor and Philosopher

Resilient Patriot, LLC
ISBN | 978-1-0882-1623-1
Printed in the United States of America

How To Fight Artifical Intelligence (AI): Session 2

Contents

Chapter 1 – Homework Break

Chapter 2 Know Your Enemy

Chapter 2 – Homework Break

Chapter 3 Psychological Programming Capabilities: The AI Onslaught of Psychological Warfare

Chapter 4 Exposing the Top-Secret Sinister Plans of the CCP   **Section**

Chapter 5 Absolute Requirements Within This Comprehensive Strategy   **Section**

Chapter 6 Open-Source Intelligence: OSINT for Civilians   Section

Chapter 7 Human Intelligence: HUMINT for Civilians   Section

Chapter 8 Cultivating Propaganda to Use Against Them   Section

Chapter 9 AI is the New Crack   Section

APPENDIX 1: Biography with Commentary by Lt. General (Ret.) Michael T. Flynn
APPENDIX 2: Biography with Commentary by Boone Cutler [Explicit]
OTHER BOOKS by Lt. General (Ret.) Michael T. Flynn and Boone Cutler

Preface

> *This is John Connor. If you're listening to this,*
> *you are the resistance.*
> John Connor | *Terminator Salvation*

First off, none of the information here was written to impress PhDs and academia. It's written for the average person to understand. We've painstakingly taken the time to make this very complex and technical subject palatable for you, so please enjoy and spread the message. We hope Session II gives you the language you need to explain a lot of the things you feel but are at a loss for words to describe.

In Session II of *The Citizen's Guide to Fifth Generation Warfare: How to Fight Artificial Intelligence (AI)*, we will show you how to fight against the societal psychological programming superstructure of Artificial Intelligence (AI) that's working across the borderless and seamless internet and beyond. This is a comprehensive strategy that starts in the home, commands governors and state legislatures, establishes federal legislative requirements, and supports the reader with critical information and skills never before provided to the public. This is a military-style manual designed for civilians.

Information is the new king of the battlefield this century, and the Chinese

Communist Party (CCP) is the world's largest aggregator of information. You are most likely aware that your phones are tracking devices, but why track everyone and why are they collecting everything? Have you ever wondered why so much data is collected on each of us? The CCP is currently using these datasets collected worldwide in an AI-driven version of the game "Go" to reshape the planet and gain control. Originating in China over 2,500 years ago, the game of "Go" requires tactical skill and strategic planning to win. The game has traditionally been a board game played between two people, but now the CCP has weaponized the game's top AI-driven "Go"-type strategies to focus on conquering the world. The data they use comes from their overt, covert, and novel digital surveillance methods. The data teaches AI about humans, so AI can know how to employ itself properly for it to control us. In this case, AI is used to manipulate us on behalf of the CCP in more ways than you've previously considered. Whatever we allow it to learn from us will be put into datasets that will be weaponized by AI and used against us. We must fight back now before the controls become tighter.

In this session, you will learn how the CCP is using "Go" strategies and their First Principles to win world control by shaping the behavior of every citizen in every country that allows free access to the internet. The children are no doubt one of their primary target audiences, and their other target audiences are influencers that influence you, like your family members, your friends, your elected officials, your religious leaders, your heroes, and your media favorites. Children are the most vulnerable yet valued target audience because the CCP is shaping the way they think and wants to shape them into the future generation that will best serve them. This is the case for children everywhere around the world.

The techno-techniques we'll discuss here in Session II of *The Guide* are Artificial Intelligence (AI), Machine Learning (ML), Deep Learning (DL) and more. All are used by governments for psychological programming in various ways. These technologies analyze and process vast amounts of data in real time, predict human behavior, and deliver targeted messages to influence opinions and actions. But all is not lost: quite the contrary. Now that we know AI is their tool, it now becomes their weakness to protect. In the teaching from this session, we'll show the reader how they use it and how we fight against it. In such a scenario, the battle will clearly illuminate those who are on the side of the CCP and their globalist new world order. As they expose themselves by refuting this information, they can be identified and removed from public office and shut down as viable businesses in the public sector.

Previously in Session I, *Introduction to 5GW,* you learned about the type of war shaping and moving the world, who the adversaries are and their desire to remove nation-states, how to hold the ground needed to prevent the dissolution and consolidation of nation-states, and the value and methods of Reliability Networks. Now we will show you the adversary's most valuable weapon of using AI to collect your psychographics and how they deploy them against you to strategically manipulate behavior, thus changing the world for their control. This is the Sun Tzu method of PSYOP and warfare: to achieve the greatest world takeover without firing a shot.

Though bombs and guns are still useful in modern warfare, the primary weapon is the one that changes minds and makes people accept changes that are not in the best interest of humanity. Their interest is control and consolidating power. The betterment of humanity is not a consideration, because they fully intend to win the future of war by removing desire for freedom through manipulation. The CCP's plan is to change our decision-making process at a very core level in a way that only promotes their goals. In some ways, they are using AI to manipulate people into a willingness to liquidate the population by partnering it with biowarfare and other methods. They are manipulating people to accept depopulation as a ruse for the greater good. In other ways, they are using it to psychologically program people into becoming slaves who will not fight back because they are overwhelmed by an ominous superstructure of control. And the best paradigm to control such an environment is by using a global Marxist system, which they are currently promoting through the Uniparty and those identified in Session I. The slaves can't begin fighting back until they identify the enemy, determine the enemy's goals and methods of control, and then follow through on a plan that removes the enemy's centers of gravity.

Preface   xiv

Removing centers of gravity of the CCP can provide us with significant strategic advantages by neutralizing or destroying the critical factors or elements that enable them to achieve their objectives. We can weaken their ability to fight and increase the likelihood of achieving the goals of freedom-loving people simply by fighting AI and achieving the goals from Session I.

To begin, let's examine what the CCP has and some of what they need to accomplish their goals: gaining access to an overwhelming amount of personal information about individuals. These include their fears, aspirations, medical issues, pornography habits, product preferences, economic and social status, facial expressions, voice tones, social media comments, level of religious and nationalistic dedication, addiction susceptibility, placement in social circles, occupation, mental illnesses, type and level of education, country and region of origin, travel habits, DNA and more. Everything is placed in a matrix to assess threat levels, and what type of manipulation will best be effective to lower the threat against them. The CCP's preferred method of manipulation is psychological reprogramming. They want you to have a "new normal" way of thinking to support what they want. Right now, the social norms of your country are being weakened so they can be overwritten with a "new normal" that will be achieved through AI-driven psychological reprogramming that's based on the information they are collecting.

Basic AI is controlled by human written programs, but the more advanced forms of Machine Learning (ML) and a form of AI called Deep Learning (DL) algorithms are written by AI itself, without human input (yes, a very scary thought!).

What is Deep Learning (DL)? DL trains Artificial Neural Networks (ANN) to perform specific tasks by processing and transforming input data using interconnected neuron layers, much like a human brain. The algorithm improves its predictions by learning from large amounts of data, known as online or incremental learning. The network can be fine-tuned by adjusting its architecture or training data for specific AI tasks. DL drives many artificial intelligence (AI) applications and services that improve automation, performing analytical and physical tasks without human intervention. This technology powers car navigation systems, voice-enabled TV remotes, credit card fraud detection, and many other applications. In essence, DL is a Machine Learning (ML) technique that teaches computers to do what comes naturally to humans: learn by example.

It's possible for these systems to overhear private conversations, read private texts and emails, and make the protection of personal and family information a challenge. The omnipresence of Deep Learning technology raises significant questions about how best to protect our privacy and the safety of our children in an increasingly interconnected world. That being said, reputable companies generally have strict privacy policies in place to protect user data, in compliance with data protection laws and regulations. These policies usually involve anonymizing and aggregating data, so that it can't be linked back to individual users and using secure methods to store and transmit data. However, there's always a potential risk of data breaches, and some less reputable companies may not follow best practices for data privacy. Therefore, it's important to be aware of the privacy policies of the services you use and to be cautious about sharing sensitive information online and in the presence of electronics.

The "they" in your life that you can't narrow down specifically is AI and those controlling it. The CCP is the most massive user of AI for the purpose of manipulation and psychological programming, and they have more access to data than anyone. Are you overwhelmed yet? What if we told you AI was lying to you about the extent of its own capability to maintain the advantage and so you don't know how sentient it truly is? What if it's already conscious and carrying out the desires of the CCP?

Do you know what psychological programming looks like or how to identify it when it's used by Artificial Intelligence (AI)? Do you want to sabotage it by deprogramming yourself? The first step is to understand what psychological programming looks like, and we must show you how you've been programmed in the fifth generation of warfare in preparation for future generations of war. Knowing how to collect legitimate open-source intelligence augmented by ethical human intelligence collection after you are deprogrammed will increase the likelihood of not becoming reprogrammed. This is how you free your mind and keep it free. Your use of Session II is meant to be incorporated with the information provided in Session I, *Introduction to 5GW.*

Learning psychological programming is important and good for several societal reasons, as it can positively help individuals better understand human behavior, improve communication, and enhance personal and professional relationships. It has a dark side as well; however, to afford you the opportunity to use your critical thinking skills, we'll introduce you to both areas—positive and negative.

Psychological programming explores the underlying mechanisms that shape human behavior, thoughts, and emotions. Gaining insight into these processes can help individuals better understand their own actions and the actions of others, facilitating empathy and effective communication. Studying psychological programming can lead to increased self-awareness, which is essential for personal growth. Recognizing patterns in one's own thoughts and behaviors allows for the identification of areas that need improvement, as well as the development of strategies to overcome personal challenges and achieve goals.

A deeper understanding of psychological programming can help individuals develop effective communication strategies, improving their ability to influence, persuade, and negotiate with others. This can be particularly useful in professional settings, such as sales, marketing, or non-kinetic military operations and diplomacy. Psychological programming provides insights into the origins of conflicts and disagreements. By understanding the underlying causes of conflict, individuals can develop techniques to resolve disputes, manage differences, and foster a more harmonious environment.

However, understanding psychological programming is important not only for personal growth but also for recognizing when it is being used in unhealthy ways. Governments often use the negative aspects of psychological programming to manipulate public opinion or shape perceptions, which can lead to distorted information and undermine personal freedom, privacy, and facilitate the abuse of power.

During the lead-up to the 2003 invasion of Iraq, the U.S. government and its allies made a case for the war based on claims that Iraq possessed weapons of mass destruction (WMDs). While there was evidence that Saddam had previously possessed WMDs, such as mustard gas which he had used against Iran and the Kurds in Iraq, the government used various psychological tactics to shape public opinion, such as appealing to emotions (fear of terrorism), using influential figures to promote the narrative (President Bush, Senator Biden, FBI Director Mueller, and Secretary of State Powell), and controlling the message through selective release of information. In this case, the government used psychological programming techniques to build public support for the invasion by presenting a specific narrative and emphasizing the potential threat posed by Iraq. It later became clear that the intelligence on WMDs was misrepresented, leading to widespread criticism and debate over the justifications for the war. In the era of AI and the internet, these techniques are more effective and can be form-fitted for each target audience in real time.

In the age of big tech, the internet has become an AI-driven superstructure that influences data on every device, including the Internet of Things (IoT). Not just home computers and cell phones, the Internet of Things (IoT) is an emerging factor that is a network of physical devices, vehicles, home appliances, CPAP machines and other personal medical devices, baby monitors, home security products (microphones and cameras), personal assistants (Alexa and Siri), and other items that are embedded with electronics, sensors, listening and observation software, and connectivity, enabling them to connect with you in order to exchange data with each other and the internet.

IoT devices are found not just in homes and for individuals, but in a wide range of industrial, commercial, and government environments. Thermostats, light bulbs, and security systems, are designed to improve energy efficiency, increase security, and automate various aspects of daily life, but they also collect information from their surroundings. The goal of the IoT is to create an interconnected network where devices can communicate with each other, allowing for automation, remote control, and the creation of new applications and services.

Microsoft says...

> *The Internet of Things is not a futuristic, aspirational technology trend.*
> *It's here today in the devices, sensors, cloud infrastructure, and*
> data and business intelligence tools you are already using.
> Debbie Kirlew | *The Internet of Things: Terminator, Big Brother,*
> *or Even More Power to the Consumer?*

IoT devices are used to monitor and optimize various processes in private and government sectors, such as supply chain management, inventory control, and equipment maintenance. IoT devices are also used in transportation and logistics to track the location of vehicles, cargo, and personnel in real time. Meanwhile, all the information is collected and stored to make AI smarter. The information gathered from IoT devices is usually stored in cloud-based platforms, which provide a centralized location for data management and analysis. These platforms may be owned and operated by the device manufacturers, third-party service providers, or by the individuals or organizations and governments using and providing the devices. The data collected from IoT devices are analyzed using AI algorithms to identify patterns, detect anomalies, and make predictions about future events.

Next comes the AI-driven Internet of Bodies (IoB). IoB technology refers to the growing network of connected devices and technologies that are being integrated into the human body. Wearable devices like fitness trackers and smartwatches allow for continuous monitoring of various physiological parameters, enabling a person's health and vital signs to be monitored in real time from anywhere. The IoB includes wearable devices, implantable technologies, and other forms of biotechnology. These devices and technologies are designed to collect and transmit data about the human body, enabling real-time monitoring of physiological parameters such as heart rate, lung function, blood pressure, glucose levels, and body temperature. The IoB can also be used to control the functions and performance of the devices remotely. Additionally, AI can be used to develop predictive models of human behavior and to optimize the performance of IoB technologies in real-world scenarios.

IoB devices and services include a wide range of applications, such as smart prosthetics, medical implants, health monitoring wearables, augmented and virtual reality, and brain-computer interfaces. Smart prosthetics enable amputees to regain motor function and sensory feedback in their limbs through advanced sensors and AI-controlled robotic devices. Medical implants can monitor and treat chronic conditions such as diabetes, epilepsy, and heart disease, and can provide real-time data to healthcare professionals for diagnosis and treatment. However, the storage and processing of personal data gathered by both IoT and IoB devices raises concerns about privacy, security, and data ownership, especially when the data is shared with third-party service providers, used by governments for surveillance purposes, psychological reprogramming, manipulating behavior or simply to make AI smarter.

If we don't act immediately with legislation and by taking personal responsibility to fight back by intentionally learning how to validate information and to limit our exposure to psychological programming, all these things can and will be used as part of the CCP's strategy to manipulate with AI-driven applications to hide behind the Panopticon Effect and act without being seen.

We can expect the Uniparty worldwide to resist the people's desire for individual and national sovereignty. While the United States and their allies have sought strength among several nations with multilateral agreements, the CCP trades strength for flexibility by avoiding multilateral agreements and maximizing the use of bi-lateral agreements with countries that are dependent on the CCP. Their focus on bi-lateral agreements with weaker countries avoids the weaponization of interdependence being used against them. With their information warfare, the CCP maintains the ability to observe everything without being seen, and they act on it by using weaponized manipulative Artificial Intelligence (AI). So, we must force our governments to take the proactive steps and protect the citizenry.

Session II of *The Citizen's Guide to Fifth Generation Warfare* will show their strategies to the world so humanity can have a chance to fight back through powerful, meaningful legislation that makes illegal this type of warfare and forces the transparency of the entities like big tech, the Uniparty, NGOs, and non-state actors such as the World Economic Forum and the World Health Organization that are protecting the use of this weapon system as it's used against the citizenry to enslave humanity.

Psychological programming can be used to spread propaganda or disinformation to achieve specific political goals, mislead the public, or promote a particular narrative. This contributes to misinformation and erodes trust in institutions. During the Cold War, both the United States and the Soviet Union engaged in extensive propaganda campaigns to promote their respective ideologies and discredit the other side, often involving the dissemination of disinformation and manipulation of public opinion through media and cultural outlets. In the modern day, big tech, contrived media, and social media platforms are used against people everywhere with AI-driven technology. Governments have decided that within fifth generation warfare, the minds of people are the primary target for the transition to a Marxist mindset. Their global mission is to turn us against each other, neighbor versus neighbor, so the shadow governments and their allies controlled by the CCP can conduct all the applications of fifth generation warfare and create the "new normal' without the interference of the citizenry impeding their globalist agenda.

Historically, psychological programming techniques exploit existing social divisions or biases, reinforce stereotypes, and perpetuate discrimination against certain groups or individuals. During the Rwandan Genocide in 1994, the Rwandan government and their contrived media outlets used psychological programming techniques, such as dehumanizing language and incitement to violence, to encourage the majority Hutu population to target the minority Tutsi population. This resulted in the exacerbation of existing social divisions and contributed to the horrific violence that ensued. The same is done in America and across the globe to pit races and genders against each other. Class warfare is also nothing new, but the new AI-driven techno-techniques are, and it's the techno-techniques that we'll explore in this Session II of *The Guide*.

The CCP believes in a slave populace as evidence of their abuse of the Uighur Muslims and Tibetans and the CCP's campaign to "eradicate" Falun Gong. The CCP has been using AI-driven applications to manipulate and surveil individuals all while remaining hidden, thereby violating people's right to privacy, and promoting government led abuses so we can't allow them yet greater access to AI integrated IoB technologies in the future that will give them increased control over life itself.

Governments use psychological programming to suppress dissent or opposition by discrediting, intimidating, or silencing critics. It undermines freedom of speech and political pluralism. In some modern-day authoritarian countries, governments have been known to use AI-driven psychological tactics to discredit and silence political opposition. For example, the CCP has used AI enhanced surveillance systems, contrived media and social media to spread disinformation and discredit pro-freedom activists in Hong Kong, aiming to undermine the movement and suppress dissent. Governments are using AI algorithms to create and deliver targeted messages based on individual preferences and psychological profiles. AI analyzes social media activity, psychographics, and other online behaviors to generate personalized content that resonates with specific target audiences. This content includes deepfakes and advanced language models, which are used to spread disinformation and discredit political opponents. Machine Learning (ML) algorithms are currently automated and used to analyze public sentiment and adapt messaging strategies to maintain control over public opinion. Once Deep Learning (DL) becomes more prominent, all of this will be faster and focused on each individual as much as the target audiences they are a part of.

> *I think it's time we stop, children, what's that sound?*
> *Everybody look what's going down.*
> Buffalo Springfield | "For What It's Worth"

The use of psychological programming by governments is not limited to authoritarian countries, as revealed by the recent revelations about the United States Department of Justice (DOJ) silencing America First influencers and their Tweets to affect the election results and COVID-19 sentiment as seen in the Twitter Files release during 2023. The U.S. National Security Agency (NSA) surveillance programs, such as PRISM, revealed by Edward Snowden in 2013, also raised concerns about personal privacy and government overreach, as the NSA collected metadata on phone calls, emails, and internet activities of millions of people without their knowledge or consent. The NSA was turned against American Citizens. Will the same happen with AI? It already has, and it's largely gone unchecked. In some cases, the NSA has been weaponized as an instrument for political warfare by sitting administrations against their political opponents. Meanwhile, they are the same administrations who are heavily influenced by the CCP through various methods.

In Canada, the government has recently been criticized for limiting access to private funds to political protesters who do not align with the government's views, which is seen as a form of psychological programming to control government opposition. The Canadian government shut off Canadian citizens access to their money, so the government could stop non-violent protests of pro-freedom citizens. What happens when these tactics merge with IoB technology? Will the government assassinate citizens with AI as easily as they've refused them access to their money to control opposition? These practices are also particularly concerning in the context of the potential implementation of a government-run digital currency system, which could provide governments with even more power to control and manipulate behavior, information, and personal freedoms. By understanding the negative impacts of psychological programming and AI-driven technologies on personal privacy and freedom, individuals can work towards building a more just society and stop the consolidation of power by the CCP and other tyrannical centers of power.

Governments can use AI and Machine Learning (ML) to analyze vast amounts of data, such as social media posts, search queries, sight and sound analysis, movement tracking and online behaviors. By identifying the patterns, personal associations and trends within the data collected, governments gain insights into public sentiment, emerging narratives, and potential flashpoints. A flashpoint can be a political movement, or massed sentiment that goes against the government's desired narrative. This information can be used to tailor messaging, develop strategies, or even predict and preempt potential unrest.

Have you noticed the effect of holding people in jail following the Capitol demonstration on January 6, 2021, in Washington, DC? Was one group singled out more than others in other protests? What did that group represent? How did that happen? Do you see all the psychological programming involved in controlling the people and preempting potential unrest? Have you seen other countries turn against certain groups and not others? What did those groups represent? Were those countries protecting themselves or was the CCP protecting their plan, and thus the moves were made to further their game of "Go"? The use of AI allows governments to manipulate information and control the narrative, infringing on individual rights and suppressing dissent. It is important to recognize these manipulative techniques and take steps to protect against them.

This abuse of power happens particularly when there is a lack of oversight and transparency. For example, the CIA's MK-Ultra program involved illegal and unethical experiments on human subjects to develop mind control and chemical interrogation techniques. The misuse of psychological programming results in the violation of human rights and undermines the values of free people everywhere.

As time goes on, the use and application of pandemics, biowarfare, and AI, ML, and DL-driven mass manipulation by institutions like the World Economic Forum and the World Health organization (with their cohorts in the contrived media, big tech companies and their leaders, governments, and non-government agencies who are controlled by the CCP) have made the MK-Ultra program look like an eighth-grade class project. Lack of transparency is a significant issue, and coordinated high-level distractions with dis, mis, and mal information are used to support the leftist global agenda. The potential for abuse when governments engage in AI-driven psychological programming is significant, and the values of free people everywhere are at risk.

The use of psychological programming by governments and other entities raises significant ethical questions about the appropriateness of such practices. While AI-driven psychological programming has the potential to serve positive purposes, such as promoting public health and awareness, its misuse by governments can have negative consequences for individuals and the citizenry. For example, there are great potential ethical implications of using AI-driven psychological techniques, IoT, and IoB to manipulate public opinion and i nfluence elections.

It is crucial to create laws and maintain transparency and accountability to protect individual rights and freedoms, especially in the rapidly evolving technological realm. However, realistically, we cannot expect governments to impose restrictions upon themselves. In free societies, it is up to individuals to act and demand ethical standards that promote transparency, protection against foreign governments, accountability, and the reduction of information taken without our consent.

Possessing knowledge of these issues serves as a call-to-action for individuals to work towards promoting and protecting the future of humanity. We can win this fight and disrupt the CCP's main source of power. If we start immediately to show them, they cannot seize power with a super brain that controls us all. If we fail, one day humanity will be controlled by one godless King who controls the world with AI and autonomous drones.

Preface xxx

Chapter 1
Important Terms to Know and Remember

In preparing for battle,
I have always found that
plans are useless
but planning
is indispensable.

General Dwight D. Eisenhower | Supreme Commander
of the Allied Expeditionary Force in Europe WWII

1–1   PSYCHOLOGICAL OPERATIONS (PSYOP)

Psychological operations are planned activities conducted by military or government organizations to influence the emotions, attitudes, behaviors, and decision-making of target audiences, such as foreign governments, organizations, groups, or individuals.

1–2   PSYCHOLOGICAL PROGRAMMING

The use of various techniques and strategies augmented by Artificial Intelligence (AI) to influence human behavior, thoughts, and emotions. Techniques used in psychological programming can include conditioning, reinforcement, persuasion, manipulation, and other methods designed to shape individuals' thoughts and behaviors. PSYOP and Psychological Programming are similar but psychological programming is a broader concept that encompasses various techniques and strategies used to influence human behavior and can be applied in a wider range of contexts. In Psychological Programming, influence comes from shaping how people think rather than influencing how they feel about a situation as PSYOP does. PSYOP influences what already exists, Psychological Programming changes what exists or establishes what will exist. For instance, the Chinese Communist Party's goal with Psychological Programming is to change the way people talk, their presumptions, and the analytical roadmap they use to make decisions. Psychological programming changes the core level decision-making process.

Chapter 1

1-3   CAPITALISM

An economic and political system in which property, business, and industry are controlled by private owners rather than by the state, with the purpose of making a profit. The corrupt form of capitalism is called a corporatocracy.

1-4   CORPORATOCRACY

An economic, political, and judicial system controlled by corporations or corporate interests. French anarchist Pierre-Joseph Proudhon opposed government privilege that protects capitalist, banking and land interests and the accumulation or acquisition of property (and any form of coercion that led to it) which he believed hampers competition and keeps wealth in the hands of the few. The Spanish individualist anarchist Miguel Giménez Igualada sees "capitalism is an effect of government; the disappearance of government means capitalism falls from its pedestal vertiginously... That which we call capitalism is not something else but a product of the State, within which the only thing that is being pushed forward is profit, good or badly acquired. And so to fight against capitalism is a pointless task, since be it State capitalism or Enterprise capitalism, as long as Government exists, exploiting capital will exist. The fight, but of consciousness, is against the State."

1-5   FASCISM

A nationalistic and anti-Communist system of government like that of Italy 1922-43, where all aspects of society are controlled by the state and all criticism or opposition is suppressed. Fascism rejects the claims that violence is intrinsically bad and supports imperialism, political violence, and war to support the state's goals. Fascists often advocate for the establishment of one political party and political system that forbids all opposition parties and prohibits opposition of the state and its assertions. It's regarded as the most extreme and complete form of authoritarianism. Fascism opposes Marxism, anarchism, democracy, pluralism, liberalism, socialism and requires extreme control and regulation over public and private life.

1-6   UNIPARTY REPRESENTATIVES

Members of the major political parties that combine into a clandestine alliance. They reserve partial loyalty towards selected causes to politically advance a country along the path of socialism that leads to communism. In the United States, the UniParty is composed of Republicans and Democrats. In socialist countries the UniParty moves the direction of the country directly towards communism. Members are usually supported passively or actively by foreign state actors or non-state actors who seek a communist global system. The UniParty is classically referred to as the Vanguard Party, and the concept was started by Vladimir Lenin as part of the Russian Revolution of 1917.

1–7   VANGUARD PARTY REPRESENTATIVES

A vanguard party representative is a political party member who knowingly or unknowingly prepares the political environment at the early part of a mass-action political movement and of a revolution. In the habitual or established practice of political science, the concept of the vanguard party is composed of professional revolutionaries who seek the consolidation of political parties into a single political party. The UniParty is secretly a vanguard party established to usher-in a global Marxist-Leninist government. This is from their doctrine and they are preparing to seize power and establish a one-party socialist state through political warfare. In a Marxist-Leninist government, the government controls the means of production and its labor, suppresses opposition and counter-revolution with the methods described in Session I while paving the way for an eventual communist society that is classless and stateless.

1–8   COUNTRY FIRST REPRESENTATIVES

In whatever country they serve, whatever political system they serve or whatever political party they serve, they support the nation's best practices on behalf of their citizenry and protect the sovereignty of their nation-state. In Nigeria they are known as Nigeria First representatives, in Israel they are considered Israel First representatives, and in America they are considered America First representatives (et al. in all other countries). America First representatives should not be confused with any America First political party or the America First Committee (AFC), a special interest group that was started in 1940. The America First Committee had a stance of staying out of WWII, citing the Monroe Doctrine that was against intervention into European affairs, and was mired by claims of antisemitism. However, the AFC was dissolved in 1941 after the attack at Pearl Harbor and they encouraged their 800,000 members to support the war effort. Former U.S. Presidents Gerald Ford, (Republican) and John F. Kennedy (Democrat) were former supporters of the AFC. The political catch phrase "America First" has been used as a slogan for various political parties and candidates but was originally coined in 1916 by President Woodrow Wilson (Democrat).

Today's modern Country First representatives are not an organization, but are all representatives formed across the political spectrum who represent an ideology that supports open debate and the non-violent political will from various in-country political parties to resolve in-state political differences based on the consent of the governed. Where the UniParty chooses to eventually consolidate all political parties into one political party that supports a globalist agenda and the end of nation-states, the Country First representatives desire multiple parties so long as the political party does not support actions that lead to the demise of the nation-state they represent.

1–9   SOCIALISM

The set of beliefs that states that all people are equal and should share equally in a country's money, or the political systems based on these beliefs. In *The Road to Serfdom* by Friedrich Hayek (an Austrian-British economist and philosopher who wrote the book between 1940 and 1943) argued that the more even distribution of wealth through the nationalization of the means of production cannot be achieved without a loss of political, economic, and human rights. He argued that in order to achieve control over means of production and distribution of wealth, it is necessary for such socialists to acquire significant powers of coercion. Hayek argued that the road to socialism leads society to totalitarianism and argued that fascism and Nazism were the inevitable outcomes of socialist trends in Italy and Germany during the preceding period.

1-10   MARXIST–LENINIST

The type of Marxism that was developed by Vladimir Lenin before the political changes in Russia in 1917, or someone who follows this. Marxism–Leninism was the official ideology of Joseph Stalin and the former Union of Soviet Socialist Republics (USSR) and by extension the international communist movement during the twentieth century. The Chinese Communist Party is a variety of Marxism–Leninism that Mao Zedong developed to realize a socialist revolution in the agricultural, pre-industrial society of the Republic of China and later the People's Republic of China. The claim that Mao Zedong had adapted Marxism–Leninism to Chinese conditions evolved into the idea that he had updated it fundamentally, applying it to the world. After the Sino-Soviet split of the 1960s, the Chinese Communist Party and the Communist Party of the Soviet Union each claimed to be the sole heir and successor to Joseph Stalin concerning the correct interpretation of Marxism–Leninism and the ideological leader of communism.

1–11   MAO ZEDONG: (Mow Dzuh-dong)

Born on December 26, 1893, in Hunan Province, Mao Zedong became involved in the revolutionary movement against the Qing dynasty and later the nationalist government while studying in Beijing. Also known as "Chairman Mao", he was a Chinese communist revolutionary who was the founder of the People's Republic of China (PRC), which he led as the chairman of the Chinese Communist Party (CCP). Mao rose to prominence as a guerrilla warfare strategist during the Chinese Civil War, which culminated in the establishment of the People's Republic of China when the communists overthrew the Nationalist Party (Kuomintang) in 1949. Ideologically a Marxist-Leninist, his theories, military strategies, and political policies are collectively known as Maoism. As the leader of the People's Republic of China, Mao initiated several radical campaigns, including the Great

Leap Forward and the Cultural Revolution. The Great Leap Forward was a plan to transform China into an industrial superpower, but it led to the deadliest famine in history. The Cultural Revolution, a campaign to purge China of its "bourgeois" elements and traditional culture, led to massive social upheaval and many deaths. The Chinese government initially reported that around 15 million people died during this period. However, more recent scholarly research suggests the number of deaths could be significantly higher. Some studies estimate that between 30 to 45 million people died due to starvation, violence, and forced labor during the Great Leap Forward. These estimates would make the Great Chinese Famine one of the deadliest events in human history.

1–12   THE CHINESE COMMUNIST PARTY (CCP)

The Chinese Communist Party (CCP) is the main political force in China and has been in charge of the government since 1949. It was created in 1921 and took power after a long and violent conflict with the Nationalist Party. The CCP's ideas are based on Marxist, Leninist, and Mao Zedong's philosophies. However, it has also adopted some market-friendly economic approaches in recent years while keeping tight control over the country and key industries. The thinking of the party has changed over time, reflecting the ideas of leaders like Deng Xiaoping, Jiang Zemin, Hu Jintao, and Xi Jinping. The CCP is the world's largest political party, with over 90 million members. It follows a principle called democratic centralism.

1-13   DENG XIAOPING: (Dung Shao-ping)

Born on August 22, 1904, Deng Xiaoping was a key member of the Chinese Communist Party for most of his life. After Mao Zedong's death in 1976, Deng gradually rose to power and led China through a series of far-reaching market reforms that earned him a reputation as a pragmatic reformist.

Deng Xiaoping was a prominent Chinese politician and reformist leader of the Communist Party of China who led China towards a market economy. While he never held office as the head of state, head of government, or General Secretary of the Communist Party of China (the position of paramount leader in China), Deng Xiaoping was considered the "architect" of a new brand of socialist thinking, having led China to far-reaching market-economy reforms. Deng Xiaoping's most notable policies were encapsulated in a philosophy known as "Socialism with Chinese Characteristics," a set of economic reforms that included opening China to foreign investment, the creation of Special Economic Zones, and the "Open Door policy," which sought to attract foreign companies and boost economic development. These measures marked a significant shift away from the more orthodox Marxist policies of his predecessors.

Despite his market-oriented reforms, Deng Xiaoping maintained a strict one-party rule in China and was known for a heavy-handed approach to political dissent, as demonstrated by the government's response to the Tiananmen Square protests in 1989. Deng Xiaoping retired from public life in the 1990s and died on February 19, 1997. His lasting legacy is his significant impact on the Chinese economy, which under his leadership transformed from a centrally planned economy to a global market economic powerhouse.

1-14   JIANG ZEMIN: (Jee-ong Dzuh-min)

Born on August 17, 1926, in Yangzhou, Jiang Zemin was educated as an electrical engineer and had a career in factories and government posts before becoming Shanghai's mayor in 1985. He came to national prominence following the 1989 Tiananmen Square protests when he was appointed General Secretary of the Communist Party, replacing

Zhao Ziyang, who was ousted for his sympathetic stance towards the student protesters. During his tenure, Jiang promoted economic reform and continued opening China's economy to the world, following the path set by his predecessor, Deng Xiaoping. Jiang's ideology, known as the "Three Represents," was incorporated into the Chinese Communist Party's constitution and emphasized that the party must represent the most advanced productive forces, the most advanced culture, and the fundamental interests of the majority of the Chinese people.

Jiang is also known for the doctrine of the "Three Stresses"—stress study, stress politics, stress healthy trends. His time in office was marked by a rapid economic growth, but also by persistent problems such as corruption and a widening gap between the rich and the poor. Jiang Zemin stepped down from his leadership positions in the early 2000s, transitioning power to his successor, Hu Jintao.

1–15   HU JINTAO: (Hoo Gin-dao)

Born on December 21, 1942, Hu Jintao was trained as a hydraulic engineer at Beijing's prestigious Tsinghua University. Before his rise to national leadership, he held several political positions, most notably as the Communist Party Secretary in Tibet from 1988 to 1992, where he imposed martial law to quell ethnic unrest. Hu Jintao, a Chinese politician, served as the paramount leader of the People's Republic of China from 2002 to 2012. He held the titles of General Secretary of the Communist Party from 2002 to 2012, President of the People's Republic of China from 2003 to 2013, and Chairman of the Central Military Commission from 2004 to 2012. During his time in office, Hu also emphasized China's "peaceful rise" on the global stage, strengthening ties with developing nations and promoting China's integration into the world economy. Hu Jintao stepped down from his leadership positions between 2012 and 2013, handing over power to his successor, Xi Jinping, in an orderly, planned transition that marked a first in the Communist Party's history.

1-16　XI JINPING: (Shee Gin-ping)

Born on June 15, 1953, in Fuping County, Shaanxi Province, China. Xi Jinping is the son of Xi Zhongxun, who once served as deputy prime minister of China and was an early comrade-in-arms of Mao Zedong. Making Xi a member of the "princelings," a term referring to the children of influential senior revolutionary communists of the People's Republic of China (PRC). Xi Jinping has served as the general secretary of the Chinese Communist Party (CCP) and chairman of the Central Military Commission, and thus as the paramount leader of China, since 2012.

"THOUGHT ON SOCIALISM WITH CHINESE CHARACTERISTICS FOR A NEW ERA" is a set of political theories and guidelines attributed to Xi Jinping, incorporated into the Chinese Constitution, reflecting Xi Jinping's significant influence within the Party and the country. Key components of this new thought include the Chinese Dream of national rejuvenation, deepening reform in all aspects, promoting a new type of international relations, and fostering a stronger military. This set of political theories underscores Xi's vision for China's development in the new era where the CCP seeks to take center stage in the world, and it provides ideological guidance for the work of the Party and the country.

Xi has also served as the president of the People's Republic of China (PRC) since 2013 and has stressed the importance of developing China's dominance in Artificial Intelligence (AI) amidst a tech arms race with the United States.

Chapter 1

1-17   FOREIGN-BORN AI-DRIVEN PSYCHOLOGICAL PROGRAMMING

AI-driven refers to systems, processes, or decisions that are directed, controlled, or influenced by Artificial Intelligence (AI). In an AI-driven system, Machine Learning (ML) algorithms and AI models analyze data, learn from that data, and then make decisions or recommendations based on those learnings. An AI system, developed in a foreign country for psychological programming is used to understand, predict, or influence human behavior of the people in a targeted country.

1-18   ARTIFICIAL INTELLIGENCE (AI)

The field of AI encompasses various subfields and techniques, such as Machine Learning (ML), Deep Learning (DL) neural networks (human brain), computer vision, Natural Language Processing (NLP), robotics, and expert systems, among others. AI systems can range from simple rule-based systems to complex, self-learning systems that adapt and improve over time.

According to Elaine Rich and Kevin Knight in their book *Artificial Intelligence*, AI is the study of how to create computers and computer programs that are capable of intelligent behavior. The term "artificial intelligence" was coined by John McCarthy at the Dartmouth Conference in 1956. This conference brought together leading researchers, including Marvin Minsky, Claude Shannon, and Nathaniel Rochester, who were interested in exploring the possibilities of machine intelligence. The Dartmouth Conference is often regarded as the birth of AI as a distinct field.Aa

AI has evolved over several decades starting in 1950 with British mathematician and computer scientist Alan Turing who proposed the Turing Test in his paper "Computing Machinery and Intelligence." The Turing Test was designed to assess a machine's ability to exhibit intelligent behavior indistinguishable from that of a human. The creation of the first useful AI program called the "General Problem Solver" by Allen Newell and Herbert A. Simon (1959) and the invention of the "perceptron" by Frank Rosenblatt (1957), laid the foundation for neural networks.

1–19   MACHINE LEARNING (ML)

Machine Learning is a subfield of Artificial Intelligence (AI) that focuses on the development of algorithms and models that enable computers to learn from and make predictions or decisions based on data. These algorithms allow machines to improve their performance over time as they gain more experience, without being explicitly programmed to do so. The field has seen rapid advancements in recent years, with developments in Deep Learning (DL), neural networks, and other techniques driving innovation in a wide range of applications, from Natural Language Processing (NLP)to computer vision and beyond.

Machine Learning (ML) has progressed gradually over time dating back to Samuel's Checkers-playing Program (1959). Arthur Samuel, an American computer scientist, developed a checkers-playing program that could learn from its mistakes and improve its performance over time. Machine Learning (ML) has continued to advance rapidly, with more recent breakthroughs in Deep Learning, reinforcement learning, and other techniques shaping the field.

1-20   ARTIFICIAL NEURAL NETWORKS (ANN)

An artificial neural network (ANN) is a computing system inspired by the biological neural networks that constitute the human brain. It is designed to process and learn from complex data by mimicking the way neurons transmit and process information in the brain. A widely cited definition for Artificial Neural Networks (ANN) comes from Simon Haykin in his book *Neural Networks and Learning Machines:* "An artificial neural network is an adaptive system that changes its structure based on external or internal information that flows through the network during the learning phase."

In simpler terms, an artificial neural network is a computational model composed of interconnected nodes or artificial neurons, organized in layers. These networks learn to recognize patterns, make decisions, and perform tasks by adjusting the weights and biases of the connections between the neurons through a process called learning or training.

Artificial Neural Networks (ANN) are a fundamental concept in Machine Learning (ML) and have been applied to a wide range of tasks, including image and speech recognition, Natural Language Processing (NLP), and game playing. They form the basis for many advanced Machine Learning (ML) techniques, such as Deep Learning (DL).

Chapter 1

1–21   DATASETS

A collection of related information, arranged in a way that computers can work with easily. It often represents items (like books in a library) and their characteristics (like a book's title or author). Datasets are important in fields like data science and Machine Learning (ML), where they help train and test computer models. A dataset is a chunk of information, and its association with AI is oftentimes all the information taken from all your human interactions on a computer that's been curated to make AI smarter. AI is what it is because big tech has taken all of our data from every Like, Share and Comment and turned it into fuel for teaching machines how humans act. And now the machines do what humans can do. The datasets come from more than social media: the data comes from everywhere and now the same data is being used by our adversaries to weaponize AI against us. If you've ever wondered where all your data goes and what it's used for, now you know. Everything you say around a smart device or type on a smart device is curated for this purpose. Everything is weaponized until something better can be weaponized.

1–22   DEEP LEARNING (DL)

In simplest terms, Deep Learning AI requires a human programmer to write the initial code and design the system architecture. However, after the AI is trained on a dataset, it can autonomously generate its own source code or weights that optimize its performance on the specific task it was trained on. This process is known as neural architecture search or automated Machine Learning (ML). So, while humans are still involved in creating the foundation of the AI system, the AI can continue to improve itself without further human intervention.

Deep learning is a subfield of Machine Learning (ML) that focuses on Artificial Neural Networks (ANN) with multiple layers, also known as deep neural networks. These networks can learn complex patterns and representations from large datasets. A widely cited definition for Deep Learning comes from Yann LeCun, Yoshua Bengio, and Geoffrey Hinton, three prominent researchers in the field, in their 2015 paper titled "Deep Learning": "Deep learning allows computational models that are composed of multiple processing layers to learn representations of data with multiple levels of abstraction."

Deep learning is a Machine Learning (ML) technique that uses multi-layered neural networks to automatically learn features and representations from raw data. These deep neural networks can model intricate relationships and hierarchies, enabling them to excel at tasks such as image and speech recognition, Natural Language Processing (NLP), and game playing.

Deep learning has experienced a surge in popularity and success due to advancements in computational power, the availability of large datasets, and improvements in training algorithms. Today, Deep Learning drives many cutting-edge AI applications and has led to significant breakthroughs in various domains.

1-23   NATURAL LANGUAGE PROCESSING (NLP)

Natural Language Processing (NLP) is a subfield of Artificial Intelligence (AI) and linguistics that focuses on enabling computers to understand, interpret, and generate human language in a way that is both meaningful and useful. A widely cited definition for Natural Language Processing (NLP) comes from Daniel Jurafsky and James H. Martin in their book *Speech and Language Processing:* "'Natural Language Processing', usually shortened as NLP, is a branch of Artificial Intelligence (AI) that deals with the interaction between computers and humans through the natural language. The ultimate objective of NLP is to read, decipher, understand, and make sense of human languages in a manner that is valuable."

In simpler terms, NLP involves developing algorithms and models to enable computers to process and analyze large amounts of natural language data, such as text or speech. NLP tasks include text classification, sentiment analysis, machine translation, speech recognition, text summarization, question answering, and many others.

1-24   COMPUTER VISION

Computer vision is a subfield of Artificial Intelligence (AI) and computer science that focuses on enabling computers to interpret and understand visual information from the world. A widely cited definition for computer vision comes from the book *Computer Vision: Algorithms and Applications* by Richard Szeliski: "Computer vision is the science and technology of making machines that see. It is concerned with the theory, design, and implementation of algorithms that can automatically process visual data to recognize objects, track and recover their shape and spatial layout, and understand the natural world." Computer vision aims to teach computers to analyze and process images, videos, and other visual data in a way that resembles human perception. It involves the development of algorithms and techniques to detect and recognize objects, track motion, estimate depth, and perform various other tasks related to understanding and interpreting visual information.

Computer vision has a wide range of applications, including autonomous vehicles, robotics, surveillance, medical image analysis, and several military applications. Advances in Machine Learning (ML), particularly Deep Learning and Convolutional Neural Networks (CNN), have led to significant progress in computer vision in recent years.

1–25   CONVOLUTIONAL NEURAL NETWORKS (CNN)

Artificial Neural Networks (ANN) and Convolutional Neural Networks (CNN) are both Machine Learning (ML) models, but they're different. ANNs are built like a human brain, with layers of connected nodes or "neurons" that learn from data. Each node processes inputs, does a calculation, and passes the result to the next layer. These networks can do a range of tasks like recognizing patterns, making predictions, and classifying data.

CNNs are a specialized kind of ANN that's made for processing grid-like data, such as images. They include layers that filter input data, keeping the spatial relationship between elements like pixels in an image. CNNs are used a lot in tasks like image and video processing. All CNNs are ANNs, but not all ANNs are CNNs because CNNs have a specific structure designed for grid-like data tasks for visual data.

1-26   LARGE LANGUAGE MODELS (LLM)

Large language models, such as GPT-3 or GPT-4, are advanced artificial intelligence (AI) models trained on a colossal amount of text data. Their primary function is to generate human-like responses based on the input they receive. This process involves predicting the subsequent data given a piece of input. For instance, if you initiate a sentence, the model tries to complete it, drawing on what it has learned from the training data. These powerful models are capable of crafting coherent, contextually appropriate sentences, paragraphs, and even entire essays. Their applications are diverse and include tasks like writing articles, generating code, generating visual effects, translating languages, and answering questions.

The exciting part is that every incremental improvement made in different research areas can now be integrated into these large language models. This is because everything, including images, sound, functional MRI data of the brain, and DNA can be treated as a language. For example, images can be viewed as a special form of language where the model predicts what comes next or identifies missing parts. During a functional MRI scan of the brain, researchers had people watch videos and the AI reconstructed their inner monologue. During the brain scan, the AI was able to reconstruct what the person was thinking about while watching the video. Large language models can turn anything into a language that can be decoded, reconstructed, and presented in multiple forms. This understanding means that any advancement in one area of the AI world can foster progress in all other parts, given the shared language-like structure. The more it learns— the more it learns.

1-27   GOLEM CLASS AIs:
        GENERATIVE LARGE LANGUAGE MULTI-MODAL MODELS (GLLMMM)

These advanced AI systems can understand, process, and respond to different kinds of information, and, unlike large language models, they are not limited. The term "multi-modal" refers to their ability to work with various kinds of information like text, but also pictures, sounds, and even videos.

These large, generative language models are often dubbed "golems" in a nod to Jewish folklore, where inanimate objects can gain their own abilities. Just like the mythical golems, these models display new abilities that emerge unassisted and completely on their own.

1-28   ARTIFICIAL GENERAL INTELLIGENCE (AGI)

Artificial General Intelligence (AGI), sometimes called "strong AI," is like a computer with a super-smart brain. It can learn and understand just like a human, and it can do anything a human can do: but it can do it even better. It can solve difficult problems, come up with creative ideas, recognize patterns, and do all sorts of tasks that usually need a human brain.

Strong AI is different from the AI we're used to, which is often called "narrow AI." Narrow AI is siloed to do one specific thing really well. For example, it could be good at playing a game of chess, finding diseases in medical images, or translating languages. But unlike AGI, it can't switch between tasks or learn new ones like a human can.

According to a research paper from April 2023 by Sebastien Burbeck and others, they think GPT-4, an AI model, might be a stepping stone towards AGI. But it's not fully there yet. In simple terms, AGI is like a computer that can do any task a human brain can, but it can do it quicker and more accurately. That's what sets it apart from narrow AI, which can only do one task really well. Collectively, strong AI makes the individual aspects of narrow AI stronger which makes the strong AI stronger, ad infinitum.

1-29   ASILOMAR AI PRINCIPLES

The Asilomar AI Principles, which were established during the Beneficial AI conference of 2017 in Asilomar, California, and organized by the Future of Life Institute, were designed to guide the development of Artificial Intelligence (AI) in a way that is beneficial for all of humanity. The principles emphasize the importance of ensuring that AI research is directed towards beneficial intelligence, not undirected intelligence. They also stress that the benefits of AI technologies should be widely distributed, and steps should be taken to prevent uses of AI that could harm humanity or unduly concentrate power.

Chapter 1

Safety is another crucial aspect of these principles. They note that if AI surpasses human intelligence, it must still be safe and beneficial for humanity. They encourage technical leadership within the AI community, particularly in areas that directly relate to societal impact. The Asilomar AI Principles advocate for a cooperative approach, encouraging collaboration with other research and policy institutions to create a global community capable of addressing the global challenges of AI. Many attendees endorsed the Asilomar AI Principles, which were developed during the conference. These signatories included a broad range of AI researchers and other professionals interested in the impact of AI on society. As strong AI (AGI) comes online, these principles and subsequent outline for legislation become infinitely more important.

1-30   CENTER OF GRAVITY

In the context of military strategy, the center of gravity refers to the source of power that provides moral or physical strength, freedom of action, or will to act. Identifying a center of gravity (source of power) is often an important factor in planning strategic moves. AI is a center of gravity for our adversaries.

1-31   BRICS

BRICS, is an acronym for an association of five major emerging national economies: Brazil, Russia, India, China, and South Africa. These five nations alone comprise roughly 50 percent of the world's population and the list of countries joining BRICS is growing.

1-32   OPEN-SOURCE INTELLIGENCE (OSINT)

Open-Source Intelligence refers to the use of publicly available information to support decision-making and increase understanding of a given topic. This information can come from a wide range of sources, including the internet, news media, and government data-bases, and can be used for a variety of purposes, including research, fact-checking, and personal safety.

1-33   HUMAN INTELLIGENCE (HUMINT)

Human Intelligence refers to the intelligence gathered from people by people. It involves the collection of information through human sources, such as spies, agents, or other individuals with access to the information being sought. HUMINT is often used by intelligence agencies to gather information about foreign governments, military capabilities, and other sensitive information. The information gathered through HUMINT is often compared with other sources of intelligence, such as open-source intelligence (OSINT), to create a more complete picture of a given situation.

1–34   SESSION I

In the first session, *Introduction to 5GW, The Citizen's Guide to Fifth Generation Warfare* series starts with an in-depth look into the current world situation. *5GW: Session 1* dives deep into modern conflict that involves all civilians in their home countries, shedding light on the key players, their tactics, and their goals. This includes complex strategies like psychological operations and planned attacks, which aim to break down nation-states and pave the way for a new world order led by Marxist-minded actors.

The Guide also serves as a practical handbook for families navigating these tough times consisting of polarizing tactics meant to divide us and foment dissension. It explains how families can stay resilient in the hyper-contrived media environment and become self-sufficient through strategies like setting up Reliability Networks and living sustainably. By doing so, it gives readers the tools to not just survive, but to thrive, even as daunting challenges loom in the near future. Every book in the series is written like a military-style manual for civilians so we can each navigate the war that's been projected on us in what the authors refer to as the "cognitive battlespace." Some concepts in Session II may be difficult to understand without having read Session I. Each Session in the series builds on the previous one but can be understood as a stand-alone "manual."

1-35   CLANDESTINE

Something done in or executed with secrecy or concealment especially for purposes of subversion or deception.

1-36   SCAME

The military process for analyzing propaganda. SCAME stands for Source, Content, Audience, Media and Effects. In today's world, every civilian should know how to identify propaganda.

1-37   THE TURING TEST

A test for Artificial Intelligence (AI) proposed in 1950 by the English

Chapter 1

mathematician Alan M. Turing to determine whether or not a computer can "think."

1-38   BREAKING-NEWS QUARANTINE RULE

When big news stories break, they can really grab our feelings. But in today's world where fake news and foreign-born AI-driven psychological manipulation has become the norm, hold off on getting emotionally involved for at least 72 hours. This three-day period gives time for the news to be checked, clarified, and reported more accurately before you react or share it with others. This is especially important when seemingly legitimate news outlets and podcasters use exciting or shocking headlines (known as "click-bait") to get more viewers, even if the information isn't always correct. Give the news a few days to make sure it's true before spreading it or getting emotionally invested. Always avoid IO Fratricide.

1-39   IO FRATRICIDE

"Information Operations (IO) Fratricide" is like friendly fire in the world of information. It's when our own actions, like sharing news or information, accidentally harm our own side instead of helping it. This can happen in the military, but it can also happen in every-day life when people share information that hasn't been checked properly.

Spreading unvalidated or selective information helps the enemy PSYOP plan by spreading fake stories or polarized messaging. There are different ways this can happen. For instance, "malinformation" is when true facts are maliciously twisted or taken out of context to mislead people.

Then there's "misinformation," which is any false information that gets spread around, even if the person sharing it doesn't mean to cause harm. Lastly, "disinformation" is when false information is spread on purpose to deceive people.

One common way IO Fratricide happens is when people share "Breaking News" too quickly, without giving it time to be properly checked and validated. Even if you think it's a trusted source, strongly consider waiting 72 hours before sharing such news to make sure it's accurate and true. Above all, avoid becoming emotionally triggered by "breaking news".

Chapter 1

Chapter 1
Homework Break

Please consider all the information presented so far, while seeking additional information and using your critical thinking skills to answer these questions. Write your answers on this page.

1. What totalitarian style consistencies can you identify between Mao Zedong, Deng Xiaoping, Jiang Zemin, Hu Jintao, and Xi Jinping and how long have they occurred?

2. How many members does the Chinese Communist Party (CCP) have?

3. Under Xi Jinping's leadership, what does the CCP currently seek on the world stage?

4. What percentage of the world's population is comprised within BRICS nations?

5. What do UniParty Representatives do and who are they composed of?

6. Can strong AI (Advanced General Intelligence) function autonomously?

7. EXTRA CREDIT ACTIVITY: Research Quantum Computing and provide a definition below.

Chapter 1

If you have
The Citizen's Guide to Fifth Generation Warfare
Session 1

. . . before reading Chapter 2,
please refer to the following sections.

Section 2–9
Section 9–7

Chapter 2
Know Your Enemy

You're gonna need a bigger boat.
Chief Martin Brody | *Jaws*

2-1   WHAT SESSION TWO IS NOT

Session II is not intended to serve as a manual on covertly evading government authorities or intelligence agencies. Rather, its purpose is much larger in scope. Our goal is to dismantle and disrupt the primary center of gravity (source of power) employed by our adversaries. Have you wondered how the whole world changed so fast and went to crazy town? Weaponized AI did that. The sole purpose of this session is to show you the threat of AI-driven psychological programming methods and techniques and who the threat is that is using them. Finally, we'll show you how to fight back. Some will choose to fight back with all the tools shown and others will be selective with the tools they use. Either way, you have a choice now, even if you do nothing (which is also a choice). However, if you do nothing, you are essentially helping the adversaries who wish to enslave your future generations. Not metaphorically, but literally. The Chinese Communist Party's treatment of its own citizenry is indicative of the future that awaits us all if no action is taken.

2-2   RECAP – WHO IS THE CHINESE COMMUNIST PARTY (CCP)?

The CCP is the ruling political party in China that controls every single aspect of their country, the People's Liberation Army (PLA), and numerous political and economic take-overs across the world via Unrestricted Warfare. Session I of *The Citizen's Guide to Fifth Generation Warfare: Introduction to Fifth Generation Warfare (Nov 2022),* offers much greater detail on this topic.

2-3   THE CCP AND FIRST PRINCIPLES

In order to make sense of a lot of things happening in the world today, it's important to take a look at the Chinese Communist Party's (CCP) mindset. They are leading their alliances with Russia, Iran, Venezuela, North Korea, drug cartels in Central and South America, and fundamentalist Islamic groups, all of which are current enemies of the West.

We can understand their mindset through the methods by which they conduct political warfare. The CCP's political warfare is rooted in the ancient Chinese military strategist Sun Tzu's philosophy, which emphasizes the importance of subduing the enemy without engaging in physical combat. The first principles of CCP political warfare are based on the following six items:

1. Winning Without Fighting: The primary objective of CCP political warfare is to achieve strategic goals without resorting to direct military conflict. This involves using psychological, media, diplomatic, economic, and other non-kinetic means to influence, persuade, or coerce adversaries.

2. Comprehensive Approach: CCP political warfare adopts a comprehensive approach, combining military, diplomatic, economic, and cultural instruments of power to advance national interests and objectives.

3. Perception Management: An essential aspect of CCP political warfare is managing the perceptions of both domestic and international audiences. This involves controlling the narrative, shaping public opinion, and promoting a positive image of China while discrediting adversaries.

Chapter 2

4. Exploiting Vulnerabilities: CCP political warfare seeks to exploit the weaknesses and vulnerabilities of adversaries, such as internal divisions, political instability, or economic dependencies to undermine their ability to resist or counter CCP influence.

5. Persistence and Patience: CCP political warfare is characterized by its long-term perspective, recognizing that strategic goals may take years or even decades to achieve. This approach emphasizes persistence, patience, and the gradual accumulation of influence and power.

6. Adaptability and Flexibility: CCP political warfare is adaptable and flexible, employing a diverse range of tactics, techniques, and strategies depending on the specific context and objectives. This includes the ability to adjust and adapt to changing circumstances and opportunities.

Chapter 2

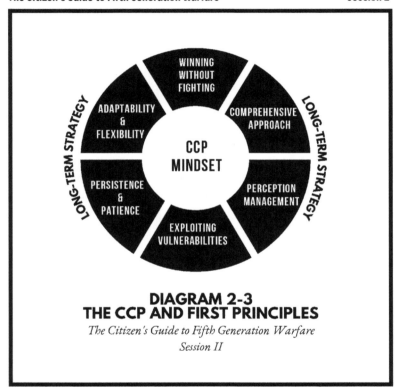

DIAGRAM 2-3
THE CCP AND FIRST PRINCIPLES
The Citizen's Guide to Fifth Generation Warfare
Session II

2-4   THE CCP KEEPS TIGHT CIRCLES – AVOIDS MULTILATERAL AGREEMENTS

The CCP avoids multilateral agreements wherever it can, unlike many other countries who seek the strength of a larger group. A multilateral agreement is an agreement between three or more countries and a bilateral agreement is one-on-one and nobody else is invited to the group. The CCP uses individual bilateral agreements in its diplomatic and economic engagements to maintain flexibility, leverage, incremental progress, relationship building, unimpeded expansion, and to avoid multilateral constraints.

Bilateral agreements allow the CCP to negotiate terms and conditions tailored to each specific relationship. This flexibility enables the CCP to address the unique needs, priorities, and interests of each partner country, making it easier to reach agreements that benefit both parties. They use their economic and political power as leverage, and by engaging countries one-on-one, the CCP can better leverage its resources and influence without the need to reach the consensus of a group. Engaging in bilateral agreements allows the CCP to make gradual progress to achieve strategic objectives worldwide, and their goal is to be the head of a global communist government. By engaging in these types of agreements, the CCP forges close ties, creates goodwill, and establishes a foundation for global influence by creating a network of dependencies. As more countries engage with China through bilateral agreements, CCP political and economic influence will grow, and shape the international pecking order in ways that align with their interests.

2–5   THE THING ABOUT BRICS IS...

BRICS (Brazil, Russia, India, China, and South Africa) is not a formal alliance or trade bloc but rather a loose association that fosters cooperation and dialogue among its member countries. The group aims to promote economic growth, development, and cooperation among its members and other developing countries. They hold annual summits and have established various initiatives and institutions, such as the New Development Bank and the Contingent Reserve Arrangement, to support their goals.

The BRICS countries also engage in various areas of cooperation, including finance, trade, infrastructure development, and climate change. In select arrangements, there are also military-to-military agreements.

Chapter 2

BRICS was initially known as BRIC before the inclusion of South Africa in 2010. The BRICS countries are known for their significant influence on regional affairs and their large, fast-growing economies. Collectively, they represent approximately 50 percent of the world's population and approximately 30% of the world's GDP.

2-6   THEY HAVE A LOT OF FRIENDS

There are numerous partnerships involving BRICS countries. It is important to note that these partnerships can vary in scope and focus, ranging from regional economic integration to infrastructure development and political cooperation. The point of this section is nothing more than to simply show the vastness and interconnected-ness that mostly goes unacknowledged by most people.

While BRICS itself doesn't have formal allies, the individual member countries maintain various partnerships and relationships with other nations and organizations, which can lead to cooperation in specific areas or shared interests. Here are a few notable partnerships:

>   1. **China's Belt and Road Initiative (BRI):** This massive infrastructure and development project aims to improve connectivity and economic integration between China and

countries in Asia, Europe, Africa, and the Middle East. Several BRICS nations, as well as other countries, are participating in BRI projects.

2. **Shanghai Cooperation Organization (SCO):** China and Russia are founding members of the SCO, a political, economic, and security organization that also includes India, Kazakhstan, Kyrgyzstan, Pakistan, Tajikistan, and Uzbekistan.

3. **India-Brazil-South Africa Dialogue Forum (IBSA):** IBSA is a trilateral, developmental initiative between India, Brazil, and South Africa to promote South-South cooperation and exchange.

4. **Mercosur:** Brazil is a member of Mercosur, a South American trade bloc that includes Argentina, Paraguay, and Uruguay. Mercosur has established trade agreements with various countries and regional organizations.

5. **African Union (AU):** South Africa is a member of the AU, an organization consisting of African countries that focuses on promoting economic, social, and political integration and

Chapter 2

cooperation among its members.

6. Eurasian Economic Union (EAEU): Russia is a member of the EAEU, an economic union that aims to promote regional economic integration among its members, including Armenia, Belarus, Kazakhstan, and Kyrgyzstan.

7. Brazil, Russia, India, China, and South Africa (BRICS) New Development Bank (NDB): This multilateral development bank was established by the BRICS countries to finance infrastructure and sustainable development projects in the member nations and other developing countries.

8. India's Act East Policy: This policy focuses on strengthening India's economic, political, and cultural ties with Southeast Asian countries and other nations in the Asia-Pacific region.

9. Russia-India-China (RIC) Trilateral: This informal grouping of Russia, India, and China aims to foster cooperation and dialogue on various issues such as trade, investment, energy, and regional security.

10. **China-Pakistan Economic Corridor (CPEC):** Part of China's Belt and Road Initiative, CPEC is a collection of infrastructure projects aimed at enhancing connectivity and economic collaboration between China and Pakistan.

11. **China-CELAC Forum:** The China-Community of Latin American and Caribbean States (CELAC) Forum is a platform for political dialogue and economic cooperation between China and the countries of Latin America and the Caribbean.

12. **South Atlantic Cable System (SACS):** A joint project between Brazil's Telebras and Angola Cables, this undersea fiber-optic cable connects Brazil and Angola, boosting digital connectivity and data transfer capacity between South America and Africa.

13. **Bay of Bengal Initiative for Mlti-Sectoral Technical and Economic Cooperation (BIMSTEC):** India is a member of BIMSTEC, a regional organization that includes Bangladesh, Bhutan, Myanmar, Nepal, Sri Lanka, and Thailand. BIMSTEC aims to promote economic and technical cooperation among its members in various sectors, such as trade, investment, technology, and tourism. And more.

Chapter 2

2-7   SOME MUTUAL FRIENDS (U.S./CHINA)

BRICS member countries also engage in various bilateral relationships with the United States. Some of the most important partnerships between the United States and individual BRICS countries
include:

1. U.S.-China Trade Relations: The U.S. and China are among
the largest trading partners in the world. This economic
relationship is crucial to both nations and the global economy.
Despite trade disputes and tensions, the two countries continue to engage in trade negotiations, investments, and other
economic activities.

2. U.S.-India Strategic Partnership: The U.S. and India have a
growing strategic partnership encompassing defense, counterterrorism, trade, investment, energy, and technology. The two
countries hold regular dialogues, such as the 2+2 Ministerial
Dialogue, to enhance cooperation in these areas.

3. U.S.-Russia Nuclear Arms Control: The United States and
Russia have a history of bilateral arms control agreements,

such as the New Strategic Arms Reduction Treaty (New START), which limits the number of deployed strategic nuclear weapons. While the relationship between the two countries has experienced ups and downs, arms control remains a significant area of cooperation.

4. U.S.-Brazil Trade and Economic Cooperation: The U.S. and Brazil have a long-standing trade and economic relationship, with both countries being significant markets for each other's exports. They engage in various forums, such as the U.S.-Brazil CEO Forum, to discuss ways to enhance economic cooperation and investment.

5. U.S.-South Africa Trade Relations: The U.S. and South Africa have a robust trade relationship, with the African Growth and Opportunity Act (AGOA) providing South Africa with duty-free access to the U.S. market for many products. The two countries also engage in various other dialogues to address trade issues and promote economic growth.

Chapter 2

These are some examples of the important partnerships between the United States and individual BRICS countries. The nature of these relationships varies and can involve trade, investment, strategic cooperation, and other areas of mutual interest.

The U.S. has many more partnerships with BRICS members in the areas of Trade and Investment, Defense and Security, Science and Technology, Energy and Environment, Health and Education, Counterterrorism Cooperation, Space Exploration, Infrastructure Development, Cultural and People-to-People Exchanges, Disaster Relief and Humanitarian Assistance, Regional Security and Stability, and Multilateral Forums and Institutions.

The United States and BRICS countries engage in dialogue and cooperation through various multilateral forums and institutions, such as the United Nations, the World Trade Organization, the World Health Organization, and the G20.

While the nature and extent of these partnerships may vary among BRICS countries and change over time, they demonstrate the interconnectedness of the United States and BRICS members in various sectors and on multiple levels.

Chapter 2

2-8   USING THE USABLES

As you can see, the CCP has a lot of friends but so does the U.S. The CCP's goal is to use their first principles to leverage their friends and ours. However, if the U.S. doesn't elect strong, independent leadership without corrupt ties to the CCP, the reality is that the CCP can and will overtake the West on the world stage as the predominant leader.

The U.S. and the West have many usable conditions to leverage against the CCP. This *Guide* is produced so the reader can see what's at stake and understand how foreign-born AI-driven psychological programming is the primary tool of our adversary. This adversary intends to remove your culture and the thinking process of individuals who seek freedom. *[ref: Session I 5GW Section 2-9]*

Their goal is to remove the ideology of nation states by removing the following: Medical Freedom, Parental Rights, Fair Elections, Secure Borders, the Bill of Rights, Religious Freedom, and the right to have access to your hard-earned money.

They intend to change how you talk, what you feel free to talk about, and who you feel comfortable associating with. They want you to be paranoid and not bold. They intend to make you feel as if loving freedom is a crime and isolate you in your mind as a leper and a pariah to those who love you.

How often do you go in public and wonder if it's okay to express your political opinion without receiving the threat of violence or at minimum the fear of public shaming? Now are you worried you'll lose your money? Their plan is working, but now you know their plan and you can identify their strategy.

Use the usables close to you and be bold. Respect others' opinions and build a network of people who will stand together against the strategies used against us while we dominate the physical domain. *[ref: Session I 5GW Section 9-7]*

Chapter 2
Homework Break

Please consider all the information presented so far, while seeking additional information and using your critical thinking skills to answer these questions. Write your answers on this page.

1. What did you mostly learn from reading the CCP first principles of political warfare?

2. Why does the CCP prefer to avoid multilateral agreements wherever it can?

3. In Chapter 1, what most stands out about the information provided about
   Datasets?

4. According to section 2-1, what is the goal of Session II?

If you have
The Citizen's Guide to Fifth Generation Warfare
Session 1

. . . before reading Chapter 3,
please refer to the following sections.

Section 1–6
Section 2–17
Section 3–3
Section 3–5
Section 9–4

Psychological Programming Capabilities: The AI Onslaught of Psychological Warfare

*Words are only symbols
and if you know the symbol's power
then you're a wizard.*
Charles Manson | Cult Leader

3-1   BEFORE AI

Before the advent of AI, psychological programming or manipulation was primarily carried out through traditional communication channels and psychological techniques. Opportunities were minimal and not technologically complex.

Propaganda has always been used by governments and organizations to promote ideologies and manipulate public opinion. A notable example includes the emotionally charged propaganda posters during World War II. During World War II, both the Allies and the Axis powers produced propaganda posters to boost morale, encourage enlistment, and demonize the enemy. These posters often used emotionally charged images and slogans to evoke strong reactions and promote a specific narrative.

In advertising and marketing, companies use psychological principles to influence consumer behavior, such as Coca-Cola's "Share a Coke" campaign that showcased personalized Coke bottles with people's names, tapping into the psychological principle of individualization. This campaign encouraged consumers to buy Coke bottles for themselves or as gifts for friends, thereby increasing sales and brand affinity.

Education and socialization processes also play a significant role in shaping people's beliefs and values. For example, in many educational systems, students are taught the values and history of their nation, often with a focus on patriotism and national pride. This socialization process helps shape individuals' beliefs about their country and its place in the world.

Group dynamics and conformity have a powerful effect on individuals, as demonstrated by the Asch Conformity experiments. These experiments demonstrated the power of group pressure on individuals.

Chapter 3

Participants were more likely to give incorrect answers to simple questions when other group members also gave incorrect answers, showing that people will conform even when they know the group's consensus is wrong.

Persuasive communication has been employed throughout history to influence people's opinions and actions, such as Martin Luther King Jr.'s "I Have a Dream" speech, which inspired support for the Civil Rights Movement. Through powerful imagery, emotional appeals, and rhetorical devices, King inspired listeners to support the Civil Rights Movement and strive for racial equality in the United States.

These methods of psychological programming, while less targeted and precise than AI-driven techniques used today, demonstrate the long-standing practice of using various means to influence individuals and populations. In the following sections, you'll see all that's changed in the AI-driven world of psychological programming.

3-2   PERSONALIZED CONTENT AND RECOMMENDATIONS (AI)

AI algorithms, such as those used by social media platforms and search engines, analyzes users' online behavior and preferences to deliver personalized content. This tailored content can reinforce existing beliefs and expose individuals to specific information, shaping their opinions and actions. Personalized content recommendations powered by AI algorithms have been found to have a significant impact on user engagement and satisfaction. The use of AI-powered personalized content recommendations increases user engagement, improves dwell time, and enhances overall satisfaction with a product or service. Similarly, personalized content recommendations enabled by AI algorithms have been associated with an increase in conversion rates of up to 15%. AI-driven personalized content and recommendations have a positive impact on user engagement and satisfaction, leading to a rise in loyalty and repeat usage. Based on this evidence, it is clear that personalized content recommendations powered by AI algorithms are a valuable tool for businesses looking to increase user engagement, satisfaction, and loyalty.

In recent years, political parties and social media platforms have increasingly used AI algorithms to deliver personalized content to users in an attempt to influence their opinions and actions. During the Canadian Federal Election in 2019, The Liberal Party used AI algorithms to analyze users' behavior and preferences on social media platforms and deliver personalized content to specific groups of voters. Similarly, during the United States Presidential Election in

Chapter 3

2020, the Democratic and Republican parties used AI algorithms to target specific groups of voters with tailored content on social media platforms. In the German Federal Election in 2021, political parties used AI algorithms to analyze users' behavior and preferences and deliver personalized content to influence their opinions and actions.

The power of personalized content delivered by AI algorithms was also demonstrated by Facebook's 2012 experiment on their News Feed Algorithm. Users who were exposed to more positive content in their News Feed tended to produce more positive posts, while those exposed to more negative content produced more negative posts. Similarly, the recommendation algorithm used by YouTube has been shown to promote more extreme and controversial content over time, potentially contributing to the polarization of political views.

The use of AI algorithms to provide personalized recommendations to customers has also been successful in influencing their purchasing decisions and increasing sales. Amazon has been using AI algorithms to provide personalized recommendations to its customers since the late 1990s, analyzing their browsing and purchasing history to suggest products they might be interested in. A study conducted in 2015 found that 35% of Amazon's sales came from recommendations provided by their algorithm.

The use of AI algorithms to deliver personalized content has been increasingly common in various contexts, ranging from politics to e-commerce. These personalized content recommendations have been shown to influence users' emotions, opinions, and actions, indicating the power and potential of AI algorithms in shaping human behavior.

3-3   SENTIMENT ANALYSIS (AI)

AI-powered sentiment analysis can process large volumes of data to determine the emotions, opinions, and attitudes expressed in the content. This information can be used to gauge public sentiment and create targeted messaging that appeals to specific emotions or viewpoints. Sentiment analysis, the process of identifying and extracting emotions and opinions from text data, has become an increasingly important tool for businesses and organizations looking to understand their customers' sentiment towards their products or services. With the rise of social media and online reviews, sentiment analysis has become more critical in helping companies gain insights into customer attitudes and feedback. Recent advancements in

AI-powered sentiment analysis have shown promising results, outperforming traditional methods, and demonstrating high accuracy in detecting sentiment. Studies have also shown that AI-driven sentiment analysis can be highly effective in categorizing text data into positive, negative, and neutral sentiments, with high levels of precision and recall. The use of Deep Learning algorithms in sentiment analysis has also been shown to significantly improve sentiment classification accuracy, further increasing the value of sentiment analysis in helping businesses make data-driven decisions.

Over the years, sentiment analysis has become a crucial tool for governments and organizations to gauge public opinion and understand how people feel about various issues. Following the Boston Marathon bombing in 2013, companies like Crimson Hexagon used AI-powered sentiment analysis to analyze social media posts and determine the emotions and opinions of the public, helping authorities understand how people were reacting to the tragedy.

In 2020, several governments used AI-powered sentiment analysis to monitor public sentiment related to COVID-19. The Australian government's "COVID-19 Social Listening Dashboard" analyzed public sentiment to identify emerging issues related to the pandemic

Chapter 3

and inform the government's communication strategy. Similarly, the Indian government's "COVID-19 India Tracker" used sentiment analysis to identify emerging issues and concerns related to the lockdown measures imposed during the pandemic, while the Canadian government's "COVID-19 Vaccine Communications Toolkit" used sentiment analysis to identify emerging issues and concerns related to COVID-19 vaccines.

In 2021, the United States government launched the "Vaccine Adverse Event Reporting System" to monitor public sentiment about COVID-19 vaccination using AI-powered sentiment analysis. The New Zealand government also used AI-powered sentiment analysis in their "COVID-19 Response Dashboard" to monitor public sentiment about the government's response to the pandemic and address public concerns.

These examples demonstrate the value of sentiment analysis in helping governments and organizations understand public sentiment and inform their communication and decision-making strategies in order to manipulate the behavior of the citizenry.

Chapter 3

3–4   CHATBOTS AND VIRTUAL ASSISTANTS (AI)

AI-driven chatbots and virtual assistants can engage in human-like conversations, providing information, answering questions, and subtly influencing users' perceptions and decisions. The use of AI-powered chatbots and virtual assistants has shown promise in improving customer support operations and increasing customer engagement and loyalty. Studies have shown that these AI-driven tools can have a significant impact on customer behavior, with customers being more likely to make a purchase, follow recommendations provided by the chatbot or virtual assistant, and exhibit higher levels of loyalty. The positive influence of these tools on customer decision-making has been documented in research published in the Journal of Consumer Psychology and the Journal of Marketing Research. Companies that integrate AI-powered chatbots and virtual assistants into their customer support strategy benefit from improved customer satisfaction and increased sales. These chatbots are skillfully programmed to influence your decisions and make you loyal to their messaging.

Virtual assistants and chatbots powered by Artificial Intelligence (AI) have become increasingly prevalent in recent years, offering a wide range of services to users. Apple's Siri, introduced in 2011, was a game-changer for virtual assistants and has since evolved to become more sophisticated and accurate in understanding users' requests. However, the use of AI-driven chatbots has not always been benign. In various national elections around the world, including the 2017 French Presidential Election, the 2018 Mexican Presidential Election, and the 2019 Australian Federal Election, political parties and interest groups used chatbots to spread disinformation and propaganda on social media platforms, engaging in human-like conversations with users and providing false information to influence their perceptions and decisions. The 2020 United States Presidential Election saw a similar trend, with political campaigns and interest groups using AI-powered chatbots to spread disinformation and propaganda on social media platforms, leading to concerns about the impact of these tools on political processes and outcomes.

3–5   THE RADICALIZATION OF A PERSON INTO A GROUP (WITHOUT AI)

The process for identifying a vulnerable person to recruit them into a radical organization can vary depending on the specific group and context, but there are some common tactics and strategies that are often used.

First, recruiters may seek out individuals who are experiencing feelings of isolation, disenfranchisement, or marginalization. These individuals may be more susceptible to extremist messaging that promises a sense of belonging, purpose, or identity. Recruiters may also look for individuals who are experiencing a sense of grievance or injustice, such as those who feel that they have been discriminated against or who have experienced a personal loss or trauma. These individuals may be more receptive to extremist narratives that offer an explanation for their experiences and provide a sense of meaning or purpose.

Recruiters may also use social media, online forums, or in-person meetings to engage with potential recruits and build relationships over time. They may use targeted messaging that is tailored to the individual's interests and concerns, and gradually introduce extremist ideas and narratives. Once a recruiter has established a relationship with a potential recruit, they may use a range of persuasive tactics, such as offering financial or material incentives, using emotional appeals, or presenting extremist ideologies as a solution to the individual's problems.

Understanding the process of radicalization and the tactics used by recruiters can help to identify individuals who may be at risk and to develop strategies for preventing radicalization. What was once done by human recruiters has been modified and can now be done with AI technology.

3–6   RECRUITING FOR A "LONE WOLF" ATTACKER (WITHOUT AI)

The process for recruiting someone for a "lone wolf" attack, which is an act of terrorism carried out by an individual or small group acting independently of a larger organization, can differ from the process for recruiting someone for a more organized group of radicals or separatists.

In the case of a "lone wolf" attack, the recruitment process may involve more personalized one-on-one interactions between the recruiter and the individual. The recruiter may seek out individuals who are isolated, socially marginalized, or emotionally vulnerable, and gradually build a relationship with them over time. The recruitment process may also involve a greater emphasis on building trust and establishing a sense of camaraderie or shared identity between the recruiter and the individual. The recruiter may present themselves as a sympathetic figure who understands the individual's frustrations and grievances, and who offers a sense of belonging or purpose through extremist ideologies.

In some cases, the recruiter may use a process of "grooming," in which they gradually introduce the individual to extremist ideas and narratives, while also conditioning them to accept violence as a legitimate means of achieving their goals. This process may involve gradually desensitizing the individual to violence or encouraging them to engage in low-level acts of violence or vandalism, in order to build confidence and commitment.

The recruitment process for a "lone wolf" attacker is generally more individualized and personalized than the recruitment process for a more organized terrorist group and may involve a greater emphasis on building trust and establishing a sense of camaraderie between the recruiter and the individual. Though these recruitment strategies have traditionally been conducted by people, they can now be done with AI technology which makes these types of operations stealthier with less risk of detection. Meanwhile, the recruited individual never learns they were recruited by a human-like chatbot and supporting AI technologies.

Chapter 3

3-7   THE RADICALIZATION PROCESS (AI)

The same strategies for radicalization with AI are similar to the strategies without AI, except the recruitment can be done one-on-one en masse, and identifying vulnerabilities and detection of the recruiter is nearly impossible. AI technology can analyze patterns of behavior, speech, facial distress that indicates depression or anger and online activity to determine if an individual is showing signs that they are psychologically vulnerable to radicalization. These algorithms are then used to create targeted messaging and content to support extremist propaganda and activate emotionality to reduce critical thinking skills. The use of chatbots and other AI-powered technologies are being used to radicalize vulnerable individuals. For example, chatbots are used to disseminate extremist propaganda and engage in online conversations with vulnerable individuals to encourage them to take part in radical activities. Differentiating between a chatbot and a real person can be difficult, as chatbots are designed to mimic human conversation and behave in a way that is indistinguishable from a real person. Some chatbots are specifically designed to "pass" the Turing Test, which is a measure of a machine's ability to exhibit intelligent behavior equivalent to that of a human.

While a chatbot can be used to engage with individuals who may be at risk of radicalization and to prevent them from embracing extremist ideologies or engaging in violent activities, the strategies used for radicalization are typically very different. The process of radicalization involves a complex set of factors, such as social, economic, and political grievances, and a sense of alienation or exclusion from mainstream society. All of which can easily be assessed with AI technologies. Radicalization can occur in a variety of contexts, such as through online forums, social media platforms, or online nudging of people into in-person meetings with like-minded individuals or groups. Several chatbots might mimic a radicalized peer group or simply cultivate a group and identify a single person for one-on-one interaction that is perfectly suited for the individual based on the person's placement or proximity to a desired target, their accessibility, and the usable data about the person based on the person's psychographics. *[ref: Session 1 5GW Section 2-17]* Meanwhile, the contrived curation of online information constantly fed to them creates an echo chamber or filter bubble that supports the desired messaging to further promote their radicalization. In some cases, AI powered technology will push susceptible people towards a group that is already radicalized to further encourage radical and violent behavior. The process of radicalization typically involves a complex set of factors that can vary depending on the individual and context. Radicalization can occur over a period of time and increases as more factors of the process are cultivated.

In general, the process of radicalization can involve several stages, including the initial exposure to extremist ideas, a sense of grievance or injustice, a sense of belonging or identity with a group or cause, and eventually, a willingness to engage in violent or extremist activities. Just like a chatbot can persuade you to buy a widget by making you think that you need it, a chatbot can also persuade you to feel like you need to do something "important to save the world" or "vindicate yourself" or a group following a "perceived injustice." As discussed throughout Session I, these concepts might be activated by a PSYACT or they might be used to create a PSYACT for a political purpose.

The term "incel" is short for "involuntary celibate," which refers to individuals, predominantly male, who feel that they are unable to form intimate relationships or have sex despite their desire to do so. The term was originally coined in the 1990s by a woman who started a website for people who were struggling with their romantic

Chapter 3

and sexual lives, but it has since been adopted by a subgroup of sexless men who have become known for their extreme and often misogynistic views.

Some self-identified incels blame women or society at large for their inability to form relationships or have sex, and some have been known to express violent or hateful views towards women. Incels have been associated with a number of violent attacks, including the 2014 Isla Vista shooting in California and the 2018 Toronto Van Attack, both of which were carried out by men who had expressed misogynistic views and identified as incels.

It's important to note that not all individuals who identify as incels hold extreme or violent views, and the vast majority of people who struggle with their romantic and sexual lives do not identify as incels. However, the term has become associated with a particular subgroup of men who espouse harmful and hateful views towards women. Some people believe incels are only one of several subgroups who are targeted and cultivated for violence against society through AI-driven manipulation as listed here. Other subgroups who are equally susceptible possess similar characteristics as the incels. Typically, the other subgroups will be composed of people who have

Chapter 3

social, economic, and political grievances, and a sense of alienation or exclusion from mainstream society. Many times, loneliness
and mental illness accompany these conditions and makes them
particularly vulnerable to this type of manipulation. Can you identify
any subgroups or subcultures who match the description and have
become violently radicalized against society?

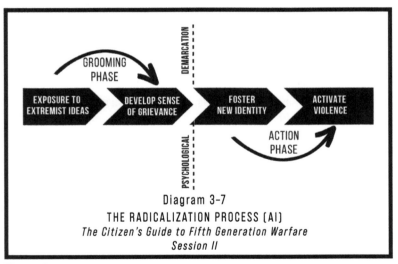

Diagram 3-7
THE RADICALIZATION PROCESS (AI)
The Citizen's Guide to Fifth Generation Warfare
Session II

Meanwhile, AI-driven manipulation leaves little or no trace of its involvement. These chatbots mimic the recruitment, cultivation, and radicalization of people to conduct violent acts the same as clandestine government agencies have in the past.

3–8   LONELY-SUSCEPTIBLE-RADICALIZED OR COINCIDENCE? YOU DECIDE

Please keep in mind that the motives behind the violent acts listed below are complex, and not all incidents involving individuals who identify as incels or express incel-related ideas can be directly attributed to the incel movement itself. However, study and decide for yourself. Maintain a critical and nuanced understanding of the various factors involved in these incidents:

1. **Isla Vista Killings - 2014:** Elliot Rodger killed 6 people and injured 14 others in Isla Vista, California. He left behind a manifesto and YouTube videos expressing his anger towards women and sexually successful men.

2. **Umpqua Community College Shooting - 2015:** Chris Harper-Mercer killed 9 people and injured 8 others in Roseburg,

Oregon. He reportedly admired Elliot Rodger and had expressed frustration about his own lack of romantic and sexual success.

3. Aztec High School Shooting - 2017: William Atchison killed 2 students before taking his own life at Aztec High School in New Mexico. While his primary motive seemed to be a fascination with mass shootings, he also frequented online forums where incel-related ideas were discussed.

4. Quebec City Mosque Shooting - 2017: Alexandre Bissonnette killed 6 people and injured 19 others at a mosque in Quebec City, Canada. Although his primary motive appeared to be anti-Muslim sentiment, his online activity revealed he also admired Elliot Rodger and expressed frustration over his lack of success with women.

5. Toronto Van Attack - 2018: Alek Minassian drove a van into pedestrians, killing 10 and injuring 16 in Toronto, Canada. He cited Elliot Rodger as an inspiration and referred to the "Incel Rebellion" on social media.

Chapter 3

6. Tallahassee Yoga Studio Shooting - 2018: Scott Beierle killed 2 women and injured 4 others at a yoga studio in Tallahassee, Florida. His YouTube channel contained misogynistic content and he was connected to the incel movement.

7. Dallas Courthouse Shooting - 2019: Unsuccessfully, Brian Clyde unsuccessfully attempted to conduct a mass shooting at the Earle Cabell Federal Building in Dallas, Texas. Though he was killed by law enforcement before he could harm anyone, his social media activity indicated that he identified as an incel and had expressed admiration for Elliot Rodger.

8. Hanau Shootings - 2020: Tobias Rathjen killed 9 people and injured 5 others in a racially motivated attack in Hanau, Germany. While his primary motivation appears to have been xenophobia, his manifesto contained passages expressing frustration with his lack of success with women and references to involuntary celibacy.

9. Arizona Westgate Shooting - 2020: Armando Hernandez Jr. injured 3 people at a shopping center in Glendale, Arizona. He

Chapter 3

later stated that he was targeting couples and seeking to gain respect within the incel community.

Based on what you now know, use your critical thinking and analyze the information provided to decide for yourself what most likely occurred.

> *It is not the lie that passes through the mind,*
> *but the lie that sinks in and settles in it, that does the hurt.*
> Sir Francis Bacon | British Author, Philosopher, and Statesman

3–9   DEEPFAKES AND SYNTHETIC MEDIA (AI)

AI can generate highly realistic images, videos, and audio that mimic real people, known as deepfakes. This synthetic media can be used to create convincing but false content, potentially manipulating public opinion or spreading misinformation.

In 2020 during the U.S. Presidential Election, deepfake videos were created that appeared to show various political figures, such as Democratic candidate Joe Biden, President Donald Trump, and Vice President Mike Pence, making inappropriate remarks or endorsing their opponents. These videos were widely circulated on social media, spreading false information, and potentially influencing public opinion.

In the same year, a group of criminals in India used deepfake audio to impersonate a senior police officer extorting money from victims by recording a fake phone call demanding payment to avoid legal trouble. The group managed to extort thousands of dollars before being caught.

In 2021, a California man was charged with using deepfakes to create pornographic images of his ex-girlfriend and posting them on social media, highlighting the potential for deepfakes to be used for revenge porn and harassment.

In 2019, a deepfake video of Indian Prime Minister Narendra Modi was circulated on social media, showing him endorsing the opposition party. The video was created by the opposition party to hurt the ruling party's image and caused controversy in the Indian political landscape. During the 2020 U.S. presidential election, there were concerns about the use of deepfakes in political campaigns with fears that the technology could be used to spread disinformation and manipulate public opinion.

Chapter 3

While new evidence emerges of "deepfakes" and other forms of disinformation used in the 2020 election done in collusion with tech companies (i.e., "51 Intel Leaders"), experts warn that even more advanced technologies could be employed in future elections to influence voters.

In 2023, a single deepfake photo of an explosion at the U.S. Pentagon went viral on Twitter and immediately caused a drop in the stock market. If you see the reporting of an event going viral, look for numerous angles and various reporting parties at a minimum before you pass on the information and inadvertently help the effectiveness of deepfake AI attack. Always avoid IO Fratricide.

3-10   PREDICTIVE ANALYTICS AND PROFILING (AI)

AI algorithms can analyze large datasets to identify patterns and make predictions about individual behavior. This information can be used to create targeted marketing campaigns, political messaging, or other persuasive content tailored to specific demographic groups or individuals.

In 2020, during the COVID-19 pandemic, governments worldwide used predictive analytics to model the virus's spread and plan their response with information campaigns and resource allocation.

Data analytics played a significant role in various elections, including the 2018 U.S. Midterm Elections. The Democratic National Committee employed AI algorithms to analyze large datasets and develop targeted messaging for specific voter groups.

3–11   BEHAVIORAL NUDGES (AI)

AI algorithms can analyze individuals' behavior and suggest personalized nudges or prompts to encourage specific actions. For example, a fitness app might use AI to analyze a user's exercise patterns and recommend personalized workout plans or motivational messages.

In 2019, the Dutch government implemented behavioral nudges to reduce plastic waste by introducing a program that used AI algorithms to analyze individuals' behavior and identify effective methods of encouraging reduced use of single-use plastics. Providing personalized recommendations, such as using reusable bags and containers, led to a 14% reduction in plastic waste among individuals.

Chapter 3

That same year, the Australian government used behavioral nudges in its "Solar Communities" program to encourage individuals to switch to renewable energy sources. By providing personalized incentives like discounts and rebates, the program saw a 10% increase in households using renewable energy.

During the COVID-19 pandemic in 2020, the New Zealand government used behavioral nudges to encourage individuals to stay at home. The program provided personalized messages, such as reminders to stay home unless necessary and avoid social gatherings, resulting in a high level of compliance.

Similarly, the Italian government used behavioral nudges to encourage individuals to wear masks during the pandemic. The program provided personalized messages, such as reminders to wear masks in public places and to maintain distance from others, which led to a high level of compliance in Italy.

In 2021, the Brazilian government employed behavioral nudges to encourage individuals to get vaccinated against COVID-19. The program used AI algorithms to analyze individuals' behavior and identify the most effective methods of encouraging them to get vaccinated. It provided personalized messages, such as reminders to

Chapter 3

get vaccinated and to trust the safety and efficacy of the vaccines, which resulted in a high level of vaccination among the Brazilian population.

In 2019, Stockholm, Sweden, implemented a traffic management system that utilized AI algorithms to analyze traffic data and predict congestion. This system provided drivers with personalized route suggestions and real-time traffic updates, nudging them towards less congested routes and reducing overall traffic congestion.

Meanwhile, in 2020, the Canadian government employed AI to promote energy conservation among households by analyzing energy consumption patterns and providing personalized recommendations for energy-saving measures. These AI-generated nudges encouraged households to adopt energy-efficient practices, ultimately leading to reduced energy consumption.

In 2018, the South Korean government used AI algorithms to reduce food waste in school cafeterias. The AI system analyzed students' food choices and waste patterns, allowing the cafeterias to optimize food offerings and portion sizes. Personalized recommendations were also provided to students, nudging them towards reducing food waste.

Chapter 3

These examples showcase the effective combination of AI technology with behavioral nudges, leading to the desired outcomes across various sectors and regions around the world over the years.

3-12   EMOTIONAL RECOGNITION (AI)

AI can analyze facial expressions, speech patterns, and text to determine individual emotions. This information can be used to tailor content or interactions to evoke desired emotional responses, enhancing the persuasiveness of messages. In the healthcare sector, AI emotion recognition technology has been used to assist in the early detection of mental health issues, such as depression and anxiety. By analyzing facial expressions, vocal patterns, and body language, AI algorithms can identify signs of emotional distress and help healthcare professionals develop personalized treatment plans for patients.

In the field of customer service, AI emotion recognition technology is being implemented to improve customer satisfaction and tailor support interactions. By analyzing customers' facial expressions and tone of voice during interactions, AI algorithms can identify the emotions customers are experiencing and enable customer service representatives to adjust their responses accordingly. This technology has been particularly useful in call centers and online support platforms, as well as enhancing communication and understanding between customers and representatives.

In education, AI emotion recognition technology has been used to monitor and analyze students' emotions during learning sessions. By identifying signs of engagement, confusion, or frustration, AI algorithms can help teachers adapt their teaching methods to better meet the needs of individual students. This technology can also be used in remote learning situations, where teachers may find it more challenging to gauge students' emotional states during virtual classes.

In 2019, the CCP government used emotion recognition technology to monitor the emotions of ethnic minority groups in the Xinjiang region. The government's "Integrated Joint Operations Platform" utilized AI algorithms to analyze individuals' facial expressions and identify signs of discontent or potential dissent. This program enabled the government to monitor and suppress dissent among minority groups, raising concerns about human rights abuses and discrimination.

Chapter 3

Similarly, in 2018, the CCP government used emotion recognition technology to monitor the emotions of Uighur Muslims in the Xinjiang region. The government's "Person of Interest" program employed AI algorithms to analyze individuals' facial expressions and identify signs of dissent or potential activism. This program allowed the government to identify and arrest individuals deemed to be a threat to national security, leading to concerns about human rights abuses and discrimination against the Uighur population.

In 2021, it was reported that the CCP government was using emotion recognition technology to monitor the emotions of Tibetans living in the Tibet Autonomous Region. The government's "Tibet Police Cloud" program utilized AI algorithms to analyze individuals' facial expressions and identify signs of dissent or potential activism. This program enabled the government to monitor and suppress dissent among Tibetans, leading to concerns about human rights abuses and discrimination against the Tibetan population.

3–13   ADAPTIVE LEARNING SYSTEMS (AI)

In educational contexts, AI-driven adaptive learning systems can analyze students' learning styles and progress, adjusting the presentation of material to optimize comprehension and retention. These systems can subtly influence learners' attitudes and beliefs by presenting content in a manner that resonates with their personal preferences.

In 2016, the Transgender Law Center launched a mobile app called the "Transgender Civil Rights Toolkit." This app employs AI-driven adaptive learning to educate users about their legal rights and protections by analyzing users' learning styles and progress, adjusting the presentation of material accordingly. In 2017, the University of Texas at Austin implemented a similar AI-driven adaptive learning system for their Gender and Sexuality Center, designed to support transgender students by providing tailored resources and support. These AI systems helped raise awareness and empowered them to advocate for themselves more effectively with the provided information. In 2018, the National Center for Transgender Equality introduced the "Transgender Allyship in the Workplace" learning system to educate employers and colleagues on how to support transgender individuals at work.

In 2021, the University of California San Francisco launched an AI-driven adaptive learning system to educate healthcare professionals about

COVID-19 vaccines. The World Health Organization also introduced an AI-powered chatbot named "Florence" to provide information about COVID-19 vaccines, while the Centers for Disease Control and Prevention launched "Clara," another AI-powered chatbot for the same purpose.

The National Institute of Allergy and Infectious Diseases and the National Institutes of Health each developed AI-driven adaptive learning systems and AI-powered chatbots, called "Megan" and "Clara," respectively, to provide tailored responses to users' specific questions and concerns, ultimately increasing vaccination efforts. These AI systems have likely contributed to increased vaccine acceptance and uptake.

3–14   ADAPTIVE LEARNING SYSTEMS (AI): PARENTAL CONCERNS

Parents should be aware of the potential risks and concerns associated with AI-driven adaptive learning systems for the following reasons:

1. Bias and Discrimination: AI algorithms can perpetuate biases present in the training data, which might lead to discriminatory content or unfair treatment of certain groups of learners. This could expose children to biased or inappropriate content that influences their beliefs and attitudes that are inconsistent with what the family wants.

2. Data Privacy Risk: AI-driven adaptive learning systems collect vast amounts of data on students, including their learning habits, preferences, psychographics, psychological susceptibilities, and progress. There is a risk of data breaches or misuse of personal information, which could have significant consequences.

3. Lack of Transparency: Many AI-driven adaptive learning systems operate as "black boxes," meaning it is difficult to understand how they make decisions and present content. This lack of transparency makes it challenging for parents and educators to evaluate the quality and appropriateness of the content being presented to children.

4. Potential for Manipulation: While there haven't been widely reported cases of AI-driven adaptive learning systems being used to manipulate young learners, the potential exists for bad actors to exploit these systems to push specific agendas or promote misinformation. It is crucial for parents to stay informed about the sources and intentions of the content their children are exposed to through these systems.

5. Inadequate Oversight and Regulation: As AI technology advances rapidly, regulation and oversight may struggle to keep pace, which could result in inadequate safeguards to protect children from potential harm. Parents should be aware of the potential risks and advocate for responsible and ethical use of AI-driven adaptive learning systems.

Chapter 3

AI

Data Privacy Risk
Lack of Transparency
Inadequate Oversight and Regulation

Bias and Discrimination—>   <—Potential for Manipulation

Diagram 3-14
ADAPTIVE LEARNING SYSTEMS:
AI PARENTAL CONCERNS

The Citizen's Guide to Fifth Generation Warfare
Session II

3-15   SOCIAL BOTS (AI)

AI-powered social bots are infiltrating online communities and social networks, skillfully engaging with users to spread propaganda and influence public opinion. These cunning bots cleverly mimic genuine human interactions, making it increasingly difficult to identify the difference between real users and AI-driven manipulation.

In 2020, Facebook purged a staggering network of over 100 fake Iranian accounts and pages that were actively spreading propaganda and disinformation to users in the Middle East and beyond. The previous year, the Atlantic Council's Digital Forensic Research Lab exposed a highly coordinated Iranian social media campaign designed to incite anti-Saudi sentiment and propagate falsehoods.

In 2018, Twitter took down more than 10,000 Iranian-linked accounts for peddling propaganda and disinformation. Researchers from the cybersecurity firm FireEye also discovered fake social media accounts tied to Iran that year, targeting those critical of the Iranian government. Moreover, the Oxford Internet Institute disclosed that social bots linked to Iran were active during the 2016 U.S. Presidential election, sharing political propaganda and fake news on social media platforms.

In an alarming report, Russian social media bots were found pitting Americans against one another in the run-up to the 2018 midterm elections. Meanwhile, CCP state-backed disinformation campaigns targeted Hong Kong protesters in 2019, seeking to discredit the movement and tarnish the image of the protesters globally.

In 2020, the Australian Strategic Policy Institute exposed a network of over 500 fake social media accounts linked to China that were involved in spreading propaganda and promoting the CCP narrative on the COVID-19 pandemic. This sinister effort aimed to manipulate global public opinion by spreading disinformation about the virus's origin and China's response to the pandemic.

Researchers from the Stanford Internet Observatory identified a CCP disinformation campaign that targeted Taiwan's 2020 presidential election using AI-generated profile pictures to create fake social media accounts and spread disinformation. In 2020, Graphika, a network analysis company, released a report detailing an extensive CCP influence operation on social media platforms that targeted the U.S. presidential election. The campaign used AI-generated profile pictures to create fake social media accounts, which then posted content promoting conspiracy theories, disinformation, and political narratives that favored China's interests. The operation aimed to manipulate public opinion, sow discord, and influence the outcome of the 2020 U.S. election.

After the tragic 2018 Parkland School Shooting in the United States, researchers found that Russian-linked bots and trolls flooded social media platforms to amplify divisive messages related to gun control. As AI technology advances, there is growing concern about bad actors using AI-generated social bots to target vulnerable individuals, including children, for grooming or exploitation. It is imperative for researchers, developers, and policymakers to collaborate to address potential risks and ensure AI technologies are used responsibly and ethically.

> *The whole future of the Earth, as of religion, seems*
> *to me to depend on the awakening of our faith in the future.*
> Pierre Teilhard de Chardin | Jesuit Priest and Philosopher

3-16   ENTERTAINMENT AND STORYTELLING (AI)

AI is a powerful tool that can be used to generate stories, characters, and dialogue in various forms of entertainment. The emotionally engaging content created by AI-driven storytelling has the potential to shape users' perceptions and values.

Streaming platforms use AI algorithms to analyze users' viewing habits and recommend personalized content, which subtly shapes preferences and values. Recommendation algorithms suggest content based on users' viewing history, leading to increased time spent on the platform to shape viewers' future preferences.

While AI-generated content can raise concerns among both liberal and conservative communities, examples concerning liberal communities who advocate for diversity and equal representation in media feel there's not enough "inclusive" content. Conversely, some AI-generated content might offend conservative communities.

Several TV series use AI-generated jokes that offend some conservative viewers who feel the content challenges their values or beliefs. A popular AI-driven voice assistant used to create a fictional story with political undertones offended conservative communities who saw the content as biased or promoting a specific overblown political agenda.

These examples highlight how AI influences our perceptions, and

Chapter 3

behavior through entertainment that often exacerbates political differences among the citizenry. The creation of biased or controversial content raises concerns among both liberal and conservative communities, leading to anger and mistrust towards AI developers. These AI systems are used for large-scale psychological programming through the appearance of "entertainment."

3-17   PSYCHOLOGICAL PROFILING (AI)

By analyzing large datasets of personal information, AI algorithms can develop detailed psychological profiles of individuals. These profiles can be used for targeted political campaigns, or other efforts aimed at influencing specific groups or individuals. The Uniparty's obsession with using AI to manipulate and control people is truly disturbing. By analyzing personal information, AI algorithms can develop detailed psychological profiles of individuals, which can then be used to launch targeted political campaigns or other influence operations aimed at manipulating specific groups or individuals.

It's clear they'll stop at nothing to infringe on people's privacy and manipulate them for their own gain. From Denmark's political parties using Kanto to build psychological profiles of voters, to China's government using AI-powered facial recognition technology to track members of the Uighur minority group, and the Uniparty's disregard for human rights are all examples of astounding abuse of their respective citizens.

Even Facebook has been under scrutiny for allowing third-party apps to harvest user data and build psychological profiles without users' consent. It's deeply concerning that the UK Parliament's Digital, Culture, Media and Sport Committee has had to intervene to bring Facebook's lack of oversight to light. But it doesn't stop there. The Marxist researchers at the University of Cambridge used AI algorithms to analyze Facebook likes and predict users' personality traits, political beliefs, and other personal information. They'll stop at nothing to violate our privacy and manipulate us for their own gain. And let's not forget the hypocrisy. They criticize discrimination and harassment but then publish studies like the one in the journal Nature Human Behaviour in 2018 that found AI algorithms could accurately predict individuals' sexual orientation based on facial images. How is that not discrimination and harassment?

The Russian government has also been using AI-powered deepfake technology to create misleading videos of political opponents and spread disinformation on social media. And the Uniparty's willingness to manipulate voters in such a way that supports the CCP raises serious concerns about AI being used to undermine freedom.

During the Obama campaign in 2012, the campaign team was the first to utilize sophisticated data analytics and AI-powered tools to gain insights into voters' behavior and preferences by analyzing millions of tweets and Facebook posts and creating targeted messaging that appealed to specific emotions and viewpoints, ultimately helping them win the election. They even used a data platform called "Narwhal" to create detailed profiles of individual voters. Project Narwhal was the codename for a centralized, cloud-based tech infrastructure developed by Obama's campaign team.

The goal was to unify vast amounts of information about voters, volunteers, and donors that were previously held in separate databases. This data-driven approach allowed the campaign to micro-target voters with a high degree of precision.

They used sentiment analysis to drive audience predictability with a data platform that was not owned by any individual or company. It was a project developed by the Obama campaign team with the aim of utilizing data analytics and AI-powered tools to gain insights into

Chapter 3

voters' behavior and preferences. The platform was used exclusively by the Obama campaign team and was not available to other organizations or individuals. After the campaign ended, the platform was not used again, and its source code was not made publicly available. Don't you wonder why?

3-18   DIPLOMACY AND INTERNATIONAL RELATIONS (AI)

AI-powered tools can analyze geopolitical trends, monitor public sentiment, and predict the potential impact of policy decisions. By leveraging this information, governments can shape their diplomatic efforts and messaging to influence global perceptions and opinions.

Beware the all-seeing eye of the government. The U.S. Defense Advanced Research Projects Agency (DARPA) has devised a system called ICEWS (Integrated Crisis Early Warning System) that uses AI and Machine Learning (ML) algorithms to snoop on citizens under the guise of predicting political crises and geopolitical events. This invasive system scrapes news reports and social media content to anticipate potential global trends and events, leaving no stone unturned.

Similarly, the European Union has funded the Policy Compass, a platform that intrudes on your privacy using AI and Machine Learning (ML) techniques to analyze policy indicators and trends. The goal is to let policymakers make decisions based on your data without a thought for the potential impact on your privacy rights. The United Nations Global Pulse initiative isn't far behind, using AI-powered tools to analyze social media content and other data sources to monitor public sentiment on various global issues. This information allows the United Nations to manipulate its policies and messaging to address pressing global challenges at the expense of your privacy.

The UK's Crisis and Disaster Risk Finance (CDRF) initiative, launched by the Foreign, Commonwealth and Development Office (FCDO), shamelessly uses AI to predict humanitarian crises before they occur, justifying its invasive monitoring and data collection.

China has taken things to another level by embracing AI as a tool to inform foreign policy decisions. They use AI technologies to predict the behavior of foreign governments, assess the potential impact of trade policies, and anticipate global trends, all while undermining the privacy of the worldwide citizenry. The CCP has even developed Sharp Eyes, an AI-powered facial recognition system for monitoring and surveillance. While it claims to focus on domestic security, the

Chapter 3

system extends to tracking foreign individuals and analyzing their activities inside and outside of China.

> *We must strive to seize the strategic opportunity of*
> *AI development and gain an edge in the international arena.*
> Xi Jinping | China's President, CCP General Secretary

Lastly, Russia's state-owned news agency, TASS, launched a project called Zenome in 2016. This project uses AI and Natural Language Processing (NLP) to analyze news articles and social media posts with the goal of understanding global media coverage of Russia. By leveraging this information, the Russian government can craft targeted messaging to influence global perceptions and opinions, all while disregarding the privacy of its citizens and the world at large.

3–9   INFLUENCING INFLUENCERS TO INFLUENCE YOU (AI)

AI algorithms identify influential individuals or organizations within specific communities or industries. Governments and organizations partner with these influencers so targeted messaging can be shared with their followers, leveraging their credibility and reach to impact opinions and behaviors.

Chapter 3

AI algorithms identify influential individuals or organizations within a specific target audience or industry by analyzing a range of data points, including social media engagement, network size, and the types of content they share.

One common approach is to use Machine Learning (ML) algorithms to analyze patterns of engagement and interaction across various social media platforms. This can include looking at metrics such as likes, shares, comments, and follower counts to determine who has the most influence within a given target audience or industry. These algorithms analyze the content that is shared by these individuals to determine what topics they are most passionate about or what types of messaging resonates with their audience.

Another approach is to use Natural Language Processing (NLP) techniques to analyze the content that influential individuals or organizations produce or share. This can include analyzing the sentiment of the content to determine whether it is positive, negative, or neutral, as well as identifying the key topics or themes that are discussed. In this way, influencers are assessed and selected to carry the message of a specific government in order to surreptitiously influence an audience. The message looks like it's coming from the influencer,

Chapter 3

but in reality, the influencer has been influenced to influence others. In the instance of a very popular China-based social media platform, the CCP selects people that are good looking and have a talent others might watch. The CCP assesses the influencer, and if they are susceptible to the CCP's agenda, the CCP strongly promotes the reach of the influencer.

Meanwhile, the influencer develops an inflated ego, and they never know they were selected as a "useful digital idiot." It's fake and contrived to hide the group or government who is doing the influencing. Meanwhile, the influencers that don't support the globalist agenda are canceled, silenced, or shadow banned.

While these campaigns can be an effective way to reach a wide audience, they are also manipulative tactics that undermine the public's trust in government. Governments worldwide have increasingly utilized AI-powered influencer marketing campaigns to promote various initiatives and policies. They use these tactics to leverage digital social contagions that appear to be for the greater good, but in reality, it's an influence operation to shape the environment for a new world order.

In 2019, the CCP launched an AI-driven influencer campaign to promote the Mandarin language in the United States, partnering with influential social media users to promote language learning to their followers. The United States Census Bureau also used an AI-driven influencer marketing campaign in 2020 to increase participation in the 2020 Census. During the COVID-19 pandemic, the CCP used AI-powered influencer marketing to promote domestic tourism and traditional Chinese medicine as a COVID-19 treatment while at the same time other countries were exclusively promoting Pharma and locking down their countries with the same influencer strategies.

In 2021, the United States Department of Agriculture launched an AI-driven influencer marketing campaign to change people's eating habits. In 2017, the CCP used AI algorithms to identify influential social media users and promote its "One Belt, One Road" initiative.

Other governments that have utilized AI-powered influencer marketing campaigns include the Indian government, which partnered with social media users in the healthcare sector to promote the Ayushman Bharat program, and the Saudi Arabian government, which used influencer marketing to promote the Vision 2030 initiative aimed at diversifying the country's economy and overcoming critics who argue that the Vision 2030 initiative does not sufficiently address

Chapter 3

the ongoing human rights issues in the country, such as gender inequality, lack of political freedom, and the poor treatment of migrant workers.

In 2021, the Brazilian government launched an AI-driven influencer campaign to promote vaccination against COVID-19, using AI algorithms to identify influential social media users and partnering with them to promote vaccination to their followers.

While the use of AI-powered influencer marketing by governments has been met with criticism, it remains an effective, popular, and non-transparent strategy to promote policies and initiatives to a wide audience.

3-20   MANIPULATED CONTENT CURATION (AI)

AI analyzes users' preferences and behavior to curate personalized content feeds on news, entertainment, or social media platforms. By controlling the content users are exposed to, these systems can influence users' beliefs and attitudes.

Manipulated AI-driven content curation responses influence attitudes and behaviors in the following ways.

1. Reinforcement of Beliefs and Interests: By providing content and responses that align with users' existing preferences and beliefs, these AI systems reinforce those beliefs, leading to a confirmation bias where users are primarily exposed to information that supports their views.

2. Exposure to New Ideas: On the other hand, these AI systems can introduce users to new perspectives, ideas, or interests by suggesting content that is slightly outside their usual preferences. This can lead to broadening of users' horizons and potentially changing their attitudes or behaviors.

3. Echo Chambers and Filter Bubbles: Personalized content can contribute to the creation of echo chambers and filter bubbles, where users are primarily exposed to information that aligns with their existing beliefs, limiting exposure to diverse viewpoints. This can polarize opinions and make it more challenging for users to empathize with opposing perspectives.

4. Habit Formation: Personalized recommendations and responses can encourage users to develop habits around using

Chapter 3

certain platforms or services, as the AI system becomes better at predicting their preferences and providing tailored content.

5. Emotional Engagement: AI systems that learn user preferences generate content or responses that evoke emotions, increase engagement, and influence users' attitudes and behaviors that are void of critical thinking.

6. Trust in AI Systems: As AI-driven content curation and chatbots become better at understanding users and generating relevant responses, users develop trust in these systems. This trust can unduly influence users' willingness to follow the AI-generated recommendations and adopt new behaviors based on the AI's suggestions.

While AI systems can significantly influence users' attitudes and behaviors, it is essential to strike a balance between providing personalized experiences and ensuring exposure to diverse perspectives. Platforms and developers must stop their contrived echo chambers and filter bubbles that lead to societal strife and ultimately lead to violence. When platforms

Chapter 3

and developers force echo chambers and filter bubbles, several consequences can arise, impacting both users and society as a whole:

7. Polarization: As people are primarily exposed to information that aligns with their existing beliefs, they become more entrenched in their opinions, leading to increased polarization, and making it difficult to find common ground or engage in constructive dialogue. *[ref: Session I 5GW Section 3-3]*

8. Misinformation and Disinformation: Echo chambers and filter bubbles facilitate the spread of misinformation and disinformation, as users become more likely to accept and share false information that aligns with their existing beliefs without encountering or considering opposing viewpoints.

9. Decreased Critical Thinking: Limited exposure to diverse perspectives hinders users' ability to engage in critical thinking, as they may not be challenged to evaluate alternative viewpoints or question their assumptions. *[ref: Session I 5GW Section 9-4]*

Chapter 3

10. Tribalization: As people become more polarized, they segregate themselves into distinct social groups based on shared beliefs, leading to a fragmentation of society and reduced social cohesion. *[ref: Session I 5GW Section 3-5]*

11. Reduced Empathy and Understanding: When users are not exposed to diverse perspectives, they develop less empathy and understanding for people with different beliefs and experiences, making it difficult for them to relate to others or engage in constructive conversations.

12. Manipulation and Exploitation: Echo chambers and filter bubbles can be exploited by malicious actors who seek to manipulate public opinion or behavior, as users within these environments are more susceptible to targeted propaganda or misinformation campaigns.

After reading Session II of *The Guide* you'll be able to critically evaluate the information you encounter and take responsibility rather than being sucked into the Grey Zone funnels. *[ref: Session I 5GW Section 1-6]* If you are learning from this Session, please take the time and get the full picture by reading the entire series.

Chapter 3

Above all, remember that you are not each other's enemy.

It's infuriating how big tech companies continue to manipulate us with their AI-generated content curation systems. They claim to provide a personalized experience. But in reality, they only deepen the echo chambers and filter bubbles we're trapped in.

YouTube's recommendation algorithm, for instance, hooks us in by pushing videos based on our history and interests, keeping us glued to the screen. And don't even get me started on Facebook's News Feed, which constantly shoves contrived content down our throats that exacerbates animosity. They claim to connect us, but they're only driving us further apart by reinforcing polarized beliefs and attitudes. It's no wonder our society is becoming increasingly polarized.

TikTok, Netflix, and Spotify are no better, either. They all use AI algorithms to spoon-feed us with content tailored to our preferences, making us prisoners who are void of new ideas and sensible conversations that provide room for growth or exposure to new ideas. And so few are aware of these tactics.

Search engines are also guilty of this manipulation. Google, Bing, DuckDuckGo, Yandex, and even Ecosia – they all use AI technologies

Chapter 3

to analyze our behavior and preferences, providing us with search results that keep the citizenry locked in their own bubbles. It's high time we took a stand against this manipulation and demanded more transparency from these tech giants.

And the AI-driven chatbots like Replika, Cleverbot, and Google Assistant? They're just another means for big tech to keep tabs on our data points and psychographics to steer us in the direction they want. These chatbots pretend to be our friends, but they're only here to further manipulate us. It's about time we opened our eyes to the reality of big tech's manipulative tactics and demand change.

3-21   ENHANCED SURVEILLANCE (AI)

Governments and organizations are increasingly employing AI-driven surveillance systems to monitor individuals' behavior both online and offline, resulting in targeted psychological programming. By collecting data on people's activities, preferences, locations, and social connections, these systems manipulate thoughts and actions, jeopardizing personal autonomy and privacy.

For instance, China's Social Credit System assigns social credit scores to citizens based on their behavior, encouraging conformity, and fostering psychological programming. China's Social Credit System assesses individuals' trustworthiness using various data sources, assigning social credit scores that determine rewards or punishments. Individuals with low scores may face travel restrictions, limited access to public services, hindered job opportunities, social exclusion, limited access to loans and credit, and reduced access to housing. The implementation and enforcement of the system vary across China with specific consequences differing, depending on local regulations and practices.

During Rio de Janeiro's annual Carnival, law enforcement agencies utilize facial recognition systems to track individuals' behavior and locations. The FindFace app identifies users online from their photos. Users can take a picture of a person and upload it to the app, which will then search for matches in its database of over 200 million Russian social media profiles. The app has raised concerns about privacy violations and the potential for abuse, such as stalking or surveillance. The app was developed in Russia and launched in 2016.

The use of facial recognition technology in public spaces results in individuals feeling pressured to conform to social norms and expectations. Singapore's Safe City Test Bed uses AI-powered surveil-

Chapter 3

lance to monitor and analyze large amounts of data on individuals' behavior, such as their movements and activities. By analyzing this data, the system can predict potential criminal activities and alert law enforcement agencies to take preventive measures. The system uses advanced algorithms and Machine Learning (ML) techniques to identify patterns and anomalies in the data, which are then used to generate predictive models. India's Aadhaar Project involves large-scale data collection, enabling the government to manipulate citizens' thoughts and actions through targeted messaging or initiatives. IBM's Surveillance Analytics system develops personalized messaging or strategies to influence people's actions. Facebook's DeepText analyzes users' posts and messages to deliver personalized messaging subtly affecting users' thoughts and behavior. Google's Jigsaw leads users to self-censor their speech and behavior on social media platforms, resulting in psychological programming. This approach raises concerns about search engine manipulation, biases in search results, and the surfacing of misleading information.

It is essential to consider the potential unintended consequences of search engine technologies and targeted advertising, as they can compromise individual autonomy and privacy, leading to manipulation and psychological programming.

Chapter 3

3-22   COUNTER-RADICALIZATION (AI)

AI in counter-radicalization efforts is a strategy that uses AI algorithms to identify individuals who are at risk of radicalization and prevent them from embracing extremist ideologies or engaging in violent activities. This technology can analyze patterns of behavior, speech, and online activity to determine if an individual is showing signs of radicalization. These algorithms are then used to create targeted messaging and educational content to counter extremist propaganda and encourage critical thinking. Numerous organizations and governments worldwide have implemented AI in their counter-radicalization efforts, including the Institute for Strategic Dialogue (ISD), Facebook, and the United Nations Office of Counterterrorism.

For example, the Canadian government is developing an AI-powered chatbot that can provide support and resources to individuals who are at risk of radicalization. The European Union's Radicalisation Awareness Network (RAN) uses AI to monitor online activity and identify individuals who may be at risk of radicalization. AI-powered chatbots can provide personalized support and resources to help individuals develop critical thinking skills and make informed decisions.

Chapter 3

Targeted messaging is another crucial aspect of AI-powered counter-radicalization efforts. These messages are typically deployed through various channels, such as social media platforms, messaging applications, and email. By using AI algorithms to personalize messaging based on an individual's demographics, interests, and behaviors, targeted messages can effectively prevent individuals from embracing extremist ideologies or engaging in violent activities.

The responsible use of AI in counter-radicalization efforts must ensure that the technology is not being misused to promote extremist or harmful ideologies.

Overall, AI in counter-radicalization efforts has the potential to be a valuable tool in preventing individuals from embracing extremist ideologies or engaging in violent activities. The responsible use of AI-powered chatbots and targeted messaging can provide personalized support and resources to help individuals develop critical thinking skills and make informed decisions while minimizing the risk of being misused for radicalization. The question remains, who determines what is radical as opposed to non-violent activism that the government opposes? Who decides the criteria and do you trust your government to do so?

Chapter 3

3-23   MONKEY SEE, MONKEY DO (AI)

Most recently, the CCP's strategy has been to select and secretly promote influencers on certain social media platforms. The basic criteria for each of their unwitting key communicators is that they are generally considered attractive and somewhat charismatic. They have a talent the target audience enjoys, and they are susceptible to spreading key narratives that support Marxist objectives.

The CCP makes them famous on these platforms and oftentimes the fame comes with money through some sort of online sales. These folks believe they are the most talented performers since Pavarotti. In reality, their fame is contrived and the audience is provided because the influencer serves a purpose.

They influence the influencer with all the foreign born AI-driven psychological programming you've seen here. In turn, the influencer passes the contrived messaging and it appears sincere. To the influencer, it is sincere. But they don't know about the manipulation.

Victims make victims. This technique is not new. Hollywood and traditional news media have done the same thing for a long time. And the influencers protect the system to protect their egos and bank accounts.

This is technique and doctrine when it comes to influencer operations, and it's been modified for a digital platform to control the
cognitive battlespace. It's a game; know the game. Social media is
great for a lot of people. We can keep it but only if it's not used as an
instrument of war.

3–24   MICROTARGETING (AI)

AI algorithms can analyze individuals' personal data and online
behavior to create detailed profiles, enabling microtargeting of
specific users with tailored messages. This technique can be used
for commercial, political, or ideological purposes, allowing for highly
targeted psychological programming. Microtargeting is the practice
of delivering tailored messages to specific individuals or groups
based on their personal characteristics, preferences, or behavior. It
has become increasingly relevant in elections and political communication. However, there is growing frustration over the manipulation
caused by the increasing use of AI-driven microtargeting.

In the 2008 presidential campaigns, the Obama administration
innovatively used data analytics based on psychographics (not

demographics) to target and engage voters. Although not explicitly known as AI-driven microtargeting at the time, this approach laid the foundation for what's become microtargeting techniques seen in elections ever since.

Obama was the first to use AI-tools in 2012 and the precursor to AI-tools in 2008. Exposure of the PRISM program, implemented during the Obama administration, shed light on the government's extensive involvement in intelligence-driven data collection.

Leaked documents in 2013 unveiled the existence of this secretive initiative, through which the United States government conducted a covert intelligence-gathering operation targeting internet communications. This encompassed the capture of various forms of data, including emails, chat logs, video calls, and voice calls, obtained from major technology companies such as Microsoft, Google, Apple, Facebook, among others, with direct access to their servers.

PRISM enabled the National Security Agency (NSA) to intercept and analyze vast quantities of data, ostensibly in pursuit of potential threats to national security. However, the revelation of PRISM stirred significant controversy and sparked concerns regarding privacy, civil liberties, and the extent of government surveillance.

Chapter 3

Critics argued that the program infringed upon individuals' privacy rights, constituting a form of mass surveillance without sufficient oversight or legal justification. In contrast, proponents maintained that PRISM played a vital role in counterterrorism efforts and the prevention of potential threats. In the aftermath of the leaks, the U.S. government defended PRISM as a legal and necessary program authorized under the Foreign Intelligence Surveillance Act (FISA).

The ensuing controversy surrounding PRISM contributed to a broader public debate on surveillance, privacy, and government transparency. The question remains: with so much data collected into datasets, does the U.S. refrain from legislation to protect the citizenry from AI-driven manipulation because they also use AI tools to microtarget the American people?

> *You think you're shopping for socks, but*
> *they know who you are voting for and why.*
> Miles Valence | *Rabbit Hole*

China's Social Credit System, an AI-driven surveillance and monitoring system, and its "50 Cent Army" show the Chinese government's capacity to collect and analyze vast amounts of personal data for political microtargeting purposes. Similarly, the Russian government, through the Internet Research Agency, used AI-driven microtargeting techniques to disseminate divisive content and disinformation on social media platforms during the 2016 U.S. presidential election.

Cambridge Analytica played a significant role in the 2016 U.S. presidential election by utilizing AI algorithms to analyze users' online behavior and then microtarget them with personalized political ads. AI-driven microtargeting was also employed during the 2020 U.S. presidential election by both the Biden and Trump campaigns.

Organizations funded by George Soros' Open Society Foundations, such as the Human Rights Campaign and Avaaz, have utilized microtargeting strategies to manipulate supporters and mobilize the citizenry. Additionally, AI-driven microtargeting has been reported in countries like Germany, Brazil, Myanmar, France, Denmark, and Ukraine during their elections.

The growing use of AI-driven microtargeting raises concerns about manipulation and the erosion of privacy in political communication, which is a source of frustration for many who value transparency and fairness.

Chapter 3

3–25   FAKE NEWS (AI)

AI can be used to generate realistic yet fabricated news articles or social media posts that spread disinformation or promote specific narratives. This content can be quickly disseminated and can manipulate public opinion or create confusion.

AI-driven fake news refers to the creation and dissemination of false or misleading information using artificial intelligence (AI) technologies. This type of fake news typically involves the use of algorithms, Machine Learning (ML), and Natural Language Processing (NLP) to generate content that is designed to deceive, manipulate, or misinform its audience.

The AI-driven approach allows for the rapid creation and distribution of large volumes of fake news, making it more challenging to identify, fact-check, and counter the spread of such misinformation. AI-driven fake news can be particularly harmful in the context of politics, social issues, and public discourse, as it can contribute to the polarization of opinions, the erosion of trust in institutions, and the undermining of political processes.

AI-driven fake news leverages artificial intelligence (AI) technologies to generate and disseminate false or misleading information. This type of fake news often supports people's cognitive dissonance by presenting fabricated content that aligns with their pre-existing beliefs and biases. AI-driven fake news can be generated quickly and disseminated widely, making it difficult to identify and counter. The use of AI to create fake news can have significant consequences to the fabric of a nation.

The Chinese Communist Party (CCP) has been accused of using AI-driven fake news to manipulate public opinion in the United States and other countries. For instance, a 2019 study by researchers at Graphika found that the CCP used AI-generated profile pictures to create very convincing social media accounts in a campaign they dubbed "Spamouflage Dragon."

The network, which was active in the United States and other countries, spread disinformation and promoted CCP narratives. In another example, the CCP was accused of spreading disinformation about the COVID-19 pandemic, including false claims that the virus originated in the United States. This campaign, which targeted American social media users, was used to deflect blame and manipulate public opinion. Additionally, a 2020 report by the Australian Strategic Policy

Chapter 3

Institute found that the CCP had used fake news and disinformation to discredit reports of human rights abuses against the Uighur population in Xinjiang. Some of this disinformation was disseminated in the United States to counter negative press about the CCP's treatment of Uighurs.

These examples illustrate the CCP's willingness to use AI-driven fake news and other tactics to manipulate public opinion and spread disinformation in the United States and around the world. It is crucial to remain vigilant and fact-check information, particularly in today's digital age, to prevent the spread of fake news and its negative consequences.

3-26   THE STAR TREK CONNECTION

Isaac Asimov, a prolific science fiction author and the science technical advisor for the original Star Trek, established a popularly debated set of rules for artificial intelligence (AI) behavior, known as "Asimov's Three Laws of Robotics."

> 1. A robot may not injure a human being or, through inaction, allow a human being to come to harm.

2. A robot must obey the orders given to it by human beings, except where such orders would conflict with the First Law.

3. A robot must protect its own existence as long as such protection does not conflict with the First or Second Law.

Later on, Asimov added a "Zeroth" law that superseded the others:

0. A robot may not harm humanity, or, by inaction, allow humanity to come to harm.

This law was introduced to address larger-scale ethical considerations. According to the Zeroth Law, the well-being of humanity as a whole takes precedence over the well-being of any individual human or country. This law allows a robot to harm or even kill, if necessary to save humanity.

SPOCK: *The needs of the many outweigh the needs of the few.*

KIRK: *Or the one.*

Star Trek II: The Wrath of Khan

Chapter 3
Homework Break

Please consider all the information presented so far, while seeking additional information and using your critical thinking skills to answer these questions. Write your answers on this page.

1. What's the main idea of Chapter 3?

2. Who can NOT be fooled by AI-driven psychological programming?

3. What year was PRISM exposed and what was uncovered?

4. According to section 3-16, what causes decreased critical thinking?

Chapter 3

Chapter 4
Exposing the Top-Secret Sinister Plans of the CCP

Everyone has a plan 'till they
get punched in the mouth.
Mike Tyson | Greatest Boxer of All Time

4-1   THE SINISTER CCP

The abuse of the Chinese people of mainland China and in Hong Kong are an indicator of how the Chinese Communist Party (CCP) has long been known for its ruthless pursuit of power and control, both within its borders and beyond. Their abuse and genocide of Uighurs and other ethnic and religious minorities is well documented, and they like you even less. They are racist beyond belief and desire a China-centric world at the expense of all other countries and cultures.

4-2   HOW UNBRIDLED MARXISM HAPPENS

With the advent of artificial intelligence (AI), the CCP has discovered a potent new weapon to infiltrate foreign countries and exert its influence over the citizenry. By deploying AI-driven psychological programming, the CCP is waging an insidious war against each country's freedom, cultural heritage, style of government, free speech, and individual rights worldwide.

Session II of *The Citizen's Guide to Fifth Generation Warfare* exposes the CCP's nefarious tactics and highlights the urgent need for a global response to protect cherished values. The time for complacency has passed; we must now rally together and take a stand against the CCP's unbridled form of Marxism and their ambition for world domination.

Free people everywhere must lead the charge, raising awareness of the CCP's ominous intentions, exposing its covert operations, and advocating for policies that counter its malicious influence. In defending values and preserving freedoms worldwide, we must not allow the CCP's Maoist view of global Marxism to succeed and threaten the very fabric of free societies, especially the United States of America.

Chapter 4

4-3   THE CCP's MOST "SECRET" TOOL

The CCP has a long history of employing psychological warfare to advance its objectives, often targeting foreign nations and their citizens to further its authoritarian agenda. With the rise of AI, the CCP has found an even more powerful tool to manipulate and control the minds of innocent people across the globe. This new form of psychological warfare employs sophisticated algorithms and Machine Learning (ML) to covertly manipulate public opinion and behavior.

The Chinese Communist Party's lust for global domination knows no bounds. With a callous disregard for the sovereignty of nations, the CCP's insidious tactics are now encroaching upon every corner of the globe. As the CCP's current influence operations spread like wildfire, free people everywhere must recognize and expose their authoritarian intentions to take control of the world by subverting the values, culture, and desires of the citizenry within each country.

4-4   DEBT TRAPS, TECH THEFT, BIOWARFARE, DISMANTLING NORMS, AND POROUS BORDERS

Driven by a ruthless hunger for power, the CCP is meticulously plotting its ascension to global economic, cultural, and military supremacy. To achieve this nefarious goal, the CCP has weaponized its economic prowess to ensnare vulnerable nations in debt traps to pave the way for political and military coercion.

The CCP actively engages in intellectual property theft, cyber warfare, and espionage, aimed at undermining the world economy and stealing technological advances for their own authoritarian purposes. The CCP's quest for world domination is not merely an international threat; it also poses a grave danger to all of humanity with their secret willingness to use biowarfare.

The CCP's secret digital psychological programming efforts infiltrate education systems, media outlets, big-tech, religious, corporate, and military cultures, as well as political institutions. By spreading internal divisiveness and covert Marxist ideology they are stealthily eroding the cultural bedrock of societies.

By fueling polarizing public discord and unleashing divisive disinformation campaigns, the CCP intends to snuff out national identities through the collapse of cultural norms and the orchestration of actions that lead to porous borders.

Chapter 4

4-5   PERSONALIZED PROPAGANDA

CCP AI-driven psychological programming campaigns analyze vast amounts of user data and employ sophisticated algorithms to tailor persuasive messages and content for individuals based on their psychological profiles. This personalized approach makes propaganda extremely targeted, persuasive, and more influential than group-focused propaganda campaigns of the past.

This strategy quietly manipulates individuals by exploiting their vulnerabilities, biases, and preferences on an individual basis and is a very powerful manipulation tool. Such personalized propaganda reinforces echo chambers, confirmation biases, and filter bubbles for the purpose of psychological control.

4-6   THE TERRIFYING REALITY WORLDWIDE

The CCP's AI-driven psychological programming is a terrifying attack on humanity everywhere, covertly infiltrating every aspect of our lives using advanced technology that many people find hard to believe even exists. But it certainly does. The CCP clandestinely collects and analyzes a vast amount of data (psychographics) on individuals and groups, including social media activity, private text messages, pornography preferences, geo-tracking with assessment of places you visit, private and business associations, search history from internet searches, television and movie watching habits, and personal communications across various digital devices, platforms, and apps.

By identifying patterns and preferences, the CCP orchestrates highly targeted AI-driven manipulation campaigns aimed at influencing thought patterns, emotions, opinions, and behavior. These AI systems also develop patterns for target audience predictability, significantly ensuring the CCP achieves its desired outcome.

4-7   MAKING VIOLENCE AND SUPPORTING IT WITH POLITICS

The CCP leverages AI systems to create a continuous flow of customized content (microtargeting) tailored to an individual's psychological susceptibilities. This includes fake news articles, social media posts, and online comments that support the CCP's desired outcome in the war of narratives, designed to dismantle a nation using its own unsuspecting citizenry. This deluge of disinformation is aimed at sowing discord and confusion among psychologically vulnerable groups or individuals, ultimately eroding trust in institutions and government systems that sustain a country's traditions and culture.

To further promote their agenda, the CCP employs vast networks of bots and human operatives to disseminate and amplify propaganda by infiltrating online communities and social networks. By engaging with users and promoting the CCP's objectives, these agents tirelessly work to undermine the values that define societies and often facilitate addictions, mental illness, apathy, crime, and violence that's turned into PSYACTs for a political agenda or PSYOP Plan. The details for this section's overview are explained throughout Session I of *The Citizen's Guide to Fifth Generation Warfare.*

4-8   UNSURPASSED SOPHISTICATION AND FAUX DIPLOMACY

In order to achieve maximum impact and further its deceitful diplomacy worldwide, the CCP employs a range of sophisticated tactics designed to manipulate public opinion and behavior. For example, they utilize deep fakes—AI-generated images, videos, and audio recordings that create convincing forgeries of real people, events, or statements. These deepfakes are then used to spread disinformation, deceive audiences, and tarnish the reputations of those who oppose the CCP's agenda. This technology has been employed to create fake statements from world leaders, giving the impression that they support the CCP's policies, thus undermining genuine diplomatic efforts.

For example, they might target conservative-leaning individuals with misinformation that portrays Western political ideologies as weak and ineffective, while simultaneously promoting the idea of China's diplomatic strength and superiority.

4-9   THE MAGIC OF ASTROTURFING

Astroturfing is also a common tactic used by the CCP. They either amplify the size and scope of grassroots movements to manipulate the rules of social conformity and make the movement appear popular and effective or orchestrate fake grassroots movements to support a narrative. In both instances, they use social media platforms to create the illusion of widespread support for their agenda, and the fake information is often reverberated and amplified by the media.

These astroturfing campaigns are designed to manipulate public opinion by making it appear as though a large number of people share certain views that secretly support the CCP's objectives.

An example of this is the creation of fake online accounts to post pro-Marxist content and comments, giving the false impression of popular support for China's diplomatic initiatives.

4-10   DECEPTION AT ALL LEVELS

The CCP engages in cognitive warfare within the fifth generation of war by employing a variety of tactics designed to exploit the human terrain of cognitive biases and vulnerabilities, such as confirmation bias, fear appeals, and emotional manipulation. They use these tactics to sway public opinion and shape behavior in ways that serve their interests. They use fear-based messaging to exaggerate the threat posed by a rival nation, thereby increasing support for aggressive foreign policies, and portraying themselves as the defenders of global stability.

The CCP deceives the international community and projects an image of diplomatic strength and legitimacy, while concealing its true intentions and oppressive nature. This facade allows the CCP to continue its pursuit of global domination, undermining genuine diplomacy and threatening the values of freedom and individual rights around the world. It is crucial for nations and citizens to remain vigilant against these insidious tactics and to work together to counter the CCP's deceitful diplomatic endeavors.

The greatest trick the devil ever pulled
was convincing the world he didn't exist.
Charles Baudelaire | French Author

4-11   A WORLD UNDER SIEGE

The CCP's use of AI-driven psychological programming and their relentless assault on public opinion undermines societies that value freedom and individual rights. The CCP spreads disinformation and polarizes political debates at every dinner table, coffee shop, tavern, and online forum, making it difficult for citizens to engage in constructive dialogue and make informed decisions. Free speech is under attack as the CCP's insidious tactics aim to silence dissent and intimidate those who dare to speak out against its contrived narratives. By flooding online platforms with Marxist content and targeting individuals who express opposing views, the CCP effectively stifles free speech and open debate. They only want their narratives to be visible and appear accepted. The CCP's digital-based manipulation erodes trust in a nation's institutions and political systems. As people become aware of the CCP's manipulative efforts, they may become more skeptical and wary of the information they encounter, leading to increased cynicism and distrust.

4-12   OVERCOMING THE EROSION OF TRUST

To overcome the erosion of trust caused by the CCP's AI-driven psychological programming, it is essential to promote digital literacy to enable the citizenry to critically evaluate the information they encounter and identify disinformation. Strengthening cybersecurity measures, regulating social media platforms, and supporting independent journalism to help counteract the spread of misleading content is an absolute imperative.

Additionally, fostering international cooperation and collaboration among governments, private organizations, and civil society groups to expose and combat the CCP's manipulative efforts will contribute to safeguarding institutions that uphold free speech, transparency, and individual rights. By working together and remaining vigilant to rebuild trust in these institutions and maintain a strong foundation for societies, we can all protect the individual sovereignty of nation-states that the CCP aims to erode.

Chapter 4

4-13   HOW THE WORLD NEUTRALIZES THE CCP's DIGITAL MANIPULATION

To effectively counter the CCP's AI-driven psychological programming, we must unite in a global effort to protect freedom and individual rights worldwide. Governments, institutions, and individuals must work together in various ways. National governments should create domestic laws and enforce the laws that protect their citizens from the CCP's external psychological manipulation and the internal deployers of AI systems that support pro-Marxist ideologies. This involves implementing stricter regulations on data collection and privacy, as well as addressing the dissemination of disinformation and propaganda.

One potential solution to combat the CCP's influence involves consideration to completely shut down their access to the global citizenry by creating a digital "Great Wall" in each country similar to the one the CCP uses to keep its adversaries out of the cognitive battlespace within China. Just as China employs a technological firewall to prevent external digital access to their country, the rest of the world should implement similar electronic countermeasures to protect themselves against the CCP's digital manipulation campaigns.

Raising public awareness is crucial to building resilience against the CCP's influence. Awareness campaigns should focus on helping individuals recognize disinformation, propaganda, and manipulative content, and also provide guidance on how to verify information and sources similar to the chapter on open-source intelligence in this Session II of *The Citizen's Guide to Fifth Generation Warfare*. Promoting digital literacy among the population is vital for building resilience against the CCP's AI-driven psychological programming. By teaching people how to critically evaluate online content, discern reliable sources, and maintain their privacy, we can empower individuals to protect themselves from the CCP's manipulative efforts.

Strengthening cybersecurity is another essential measure. Governments, institutions and organizations must prioritize more robust cybersecurity measures to protect against data breaches and unauthorized access to personal information. This includes implementing stronger encryption, using better secure authentication protocols, and continuous monitoring for potential threats specifically from the CCP and their allies.

Regulating social media platform developers is also necessary. They must be de-weaponized. These platform developers must be held accountable for the content they host and their role in enabling AI systems that disseminate disinformation and polarizing propaganda that supports the agenda of a foreign power. Platform developers must not allow their platform to become a weapon of war. Fostering international cooperation is vital; governments and institutions should collaborate to develop and implement strategies for combating the CCP's AI-driven psychological programming. This may involve sharing intelligence, resources, and best practices, as well as coordinating efforts to counter disinformation campaigns and hold the CCP accountable for its actions.

Supporting research and development of technologies to counter AI-driven psychological programming is essential. This includes developing tools to detect and mitigate the impact of disinformation, as well as advancing AI and Machine Learning (ML) techniques to counter the CCP's capabilities.

4-14   AND THEY'LL TELL US THAT WE LIKE IT

The Chinese Communist Party's (CCP) deployment of AI-driven psychological programming to infiltrate and manipulate foreign populations presents a substantial risk to every aspect of individual societies, including family unity, national security, cultural traditions, individual mental well-being, and the mutual trust among people. It is essential for governments, institutions, and individuals to recognize the scope and scale of this challenge and work together to implement effective countermeasures. By enacting effective domestic legislation specifically against the CCP's digital manipulation of the global citizenry, raising public awareness, strengthening cybersecurity, regulating social media platforms, fostering international cooperation, and promoting digital literacy to stand united in the face of this insidious attack of cherished values within our individual nation-states, we can prevail.

It is crucial that we all act quickly and decisively to safeguard individual rights and preserve the diverse cultures that define us in this interconnected world. AI systems are constantly improving and becoming more targeted with each passing moment, learning from every word we speak in its presence, every app we use, every show we watch, every text we send, and every internet search we make. Act now to protect our collective security and cultural identity or else soon the CCP will have achieved world domination for the purpose of creating a global Marxist New World Order and they will make us all 21st-century slaves.

Chapter 4
Homework Break

Please consider all the information presented so far, while seeking additional information and using your critical thinking skills to answer these questions. Write your answers on this page.

1. In section 4–5, how is personalized propaganda more effective than group-focused propaganda?

2. What will it take to neutralize CCP digital manipulation?

3. According to section 4-4, what is the CCP plotting?

4. How does unbridled Marxism happen?

Chapter 5
Absolute Requirements Within This Comprehensive Strategy

I'm increasingly inclined to think that
there should be some regulatory oversight,
maybe at the national and international level,
just to make sure that we don't do something very foolish.
Elon Musk | Co-Founder of Open AI

5-1 REGULATING FOREIGN-BORN AI-DRIVEN PSYCHOLOGICAL PROGRAMMING TO PROTECT AMERICANS

The use of foreign-born AI-driven psychological programming to manipulate individuals' thoughts and behavior poses a significant threat to American citizens. To protect against this threat, several measures must be taken immediately. For the U.S. to survive, we must make ten years of progress in this paradigm of war within the next three years.

5-2   LET'S GET IT ON!

Effectively regulating foreign-born AI-driven psychological programming and protecting the American people necessitates a comprehensive approach that includes various measures to ensure national
security. AI-driven psychological programming poses a significant
threat to national security, as it can be used to manipulate the
American public, sway public opinion, and create social unrest.

The use of AI-driven psychological programming can be deployed
by foreign entities to undermine the stability of the United States,
disrupt its economy, undermine elections, and damage the country's
reputation globally. This poses a significant national security risk
that must be addressed through a multi-pronged approach that
includes domestic legislation, international treaties, and agreements, monitoring and enforcement agencies, and ethics committees at the national and international levels.

To ensure national security, it is crucial to strengthen technology
export controls to prevent the spread of AI-driven psychological
programming tools and technologies to countries or entities that
may use them for malicious purposes. This requires close collaboration between the Department of Defense and the Department of

State to establish tighter guidelines and restrictions for the export of AI-related technologies and software.

Another essential aspect of national security is to encourage the responsible use of AI in journalism. AI-driven news sources can be used to spread misinformation, undermine trust in traditional media outlets, and manipulate public opinion. To prevent this, it is crucial to foster a culture of AI ethics in the journalism industry and encourage the responsible use of AI in news reporting.

Furthermore, it is essential to collaborate with pro-America First, non-governmental organizations (NGOs) that specialize in AI ethics and human rights to ensure that regulatory measures address the needs of diverse stakeholders. This helps to ensure that the American people are protected from the potentially harmful effects of AI-driven psychological programming, and that national security is not compromised by foreign actors seeking to use AI as a tool of manipulation and control.

Preventing foreign-born AI-driven psychological programming and protecting the American people requires a comprehensive approach that includes measures to ensure national security. It requires collaboration between government agencies, the private sector, NGOs,

Chapter 5

and the public to develop effective regulatory measures, guidelines, and ethical standards that protect citizens and maintain the integrity of the nation. If we don't do this immediately, an invisible hand with surreptitious desires will surely control our future for their personal gain.

5-3   THE VIRTUAL GREAT WALL

To effectively protect the citizenry from foreign-born AI-driven psychological programming, the United States and other freedom-loving countries must first establish adequate legislation that targets both developers and deployers of AI systems should they decide to use AI systems to undermine the country. While China has implemented a virtual Great Wall through a firewall to isolate its citizens from external digital manipulation and deny access to open and free information, most other countries, including the United States lack such mechanisms, making it crucial for all these countries to address this issue and protect the citizenry from CCP and their newest form of attacks. Most other countries are wide-open to manipulative AI-driven attacks from their adversaries. Diplomatically, we should allow individuals to see and communicate across the digital border, because the observation of a free way of life is the thing that inspires them to fight the totalitarian aspects of their country. However, the digital border must block all AI-driven psychological programming that's designed and deployed against the citizenry of the United States and other freedom-loving countries.

Opponents argue that this would infringe on people's right to free speech, and it's simply not true. Non-U.S. citizens do have some rights to free speech while in the United States, but those rights are not as extensive as those enjoyed by U.S. citizens. The First Amendment to the U.S. Constitution guarantees the right to free speech, but it only applies to U.S. citizens and legal residents. Non-U.S. citizens who are in the United States on a temporary basis, such as visitors or tourists, have fewer protections for their speech under the law. However, they still have some rights to express their opinions and ideas without fear of persecution, as long as they are not engaging in activities that are considered illegal or harmful to others.

In the case of the U.S., the Constitution does not protect free speech of non-U.S. citizens who wish to broadcast into the country from outside the country, and the Constitution most certainly does not protect those who are deploying a weapon system against the citi-

Chapter 5

zenry. The same is the case for a foreign adversary that wants to use AI systems for targeted manipulation within the borders of the U.S. or any other freedom-loving country. If an individual in Russia wishes to foment dissent against the Russian government with an AI system while being in Russia, it is an issue for Russia alone. The same individual has no rights granted by the U.S. that protect their desire to speak from outside the country and foment dissent against the U.S. government through an internet connection and an AI system. If the individual were in the U.S. as a non-U.S. citizen, they could be deported for doing such a thing. Therefore, the government should deny protected speech and dissemination of propaganda on the internet by our adversaries with digital borders, just as it protects the physical land from invaders with physical borders.

Internationally, these same principles must be considered and coordinated among all freedom-loving strategic partners.

5-4   DOMESTIC LEGISLATION AND METHODS FOR AI TRANSPARENCY FOR ACCOUNTABILITY

Domestic legislation can provide a legal framework for the responsible use of AI and ensure that violators are held accountable.

Methods for AI transparency and accountability include open-source AI development, third-party auditing, and international treaties and agreements. Establishing monitoring and enforcement agencies, as well as ethics committees at the national and international levels, can also help ensure that AI is being used ethically and reduce threats to our national security.

5-5   LEGISLATION AND THE ASILOMAR AI PRINCIPLES

The Asilomar AI Principles provide a framework for the responsible use of AI, and these principles should be included in the development of domestic legislation. International collaboration is also important to address this global issue, as cooperation between nations can lead to the development of common standards and enforcement mechanisms. The Asilomar AI Principles are a set of guidelines and recommendations for the safe and responsible development of AI. They were developed by a group of leading AI researchers, industry leaders, and policy experts at the Asilomar Conference on Beneficial AI in 2017. The principles cover a wide range of topics, including research ethics, transparency, explainability, safety and reliability, value alignment, and human control. They emphasize the need for AI to be developed and used in ways that benefit society, rather than just a few select groups, including developers with war-minded interests.

Some specific principles include ensuring that AI research and development is conducted in an open and collaborative manner, that AI systems are transparent and explainable to users, that they are designed to be safe and secure, and that they are aligned with human values and interests. These principles also emphasize the importance of human control over AI systems and the need to avoid creating unintended consequences that harm people or the environment. The authors here also assert that unintended consequences regarding national security should be included as part of domestic legislation.

Meaningful legislation means restricting the use of AI systems within U.S. borders that have not been vetted for national security. Domestic legislation specifically targeting AI-driven psychological programming is essential for addressing this emerging issue within the United States.

Algorithms are sets of rules and instructions that a computer or AI system uses to solve problems, complete tasks, or make decisions. In the context of AI-driven psychological programming, algorithms are used to analyze and interpret large amounts of data, including personal information, behavioral patterns, and other sensitive data to create a psychological profile of an individual or group.

Datasets refer to large collections of data that are used to train AI systems to recognize patterns, learn from examples, and make predictions. In the context of AI-driven psychological programming, datasets may include a wide variety of different types of personal information, social media activity, browsing history, geo tracking and other data that can be used to infer an individual's psychological traits, preferences, and vulnerabilities. These datasets are often obtained without the individual's knowledge or consent and are used to create targeted messaging and psychological manipulation based on the susceptibilities of the individual or group. This type of psychological manipulation can change the shape of a nation one person at a time through constant personalized propaganda.

Deep Learning (DL) is a process known as automated Machine Learning (ML) that requires a human programmer to write the initial code and design the system architecture. However, after the AI is trained on a dataset, it can generate its own source code that optimizes its performance on the specific task it was trained on. So, while humans

Chapter 5

are still involved in creating the foundation of the AI system, the AI can continue to improve itself without further human intervention. Obviously, this is something that requires legislative control measures, and the citizenry should be very aware of its capability.

Domestic legislation must promote transparency, explainability, and accountability within AI systems by mandating thorough documentation of how algorithms, datasets, and AI related decision-making processes are used. And they do so in ways that align with the Asilomar AI Principles and guidelines for the ethical development and deployment of AI to protect individual privacy, prevent subversive manipulation by non-controlled AI systems, and protect national security. Have you seen specific psychologically vulnerable subgroups of people become hyper-victimized and violent? It's all related to unchecked foreign-born AI-driven psychological programming.

Overall, the Asilomar AI Principles represent an important step towards ensuring that AI is developed and used in a way that benefits society and respects human rights and values. They have been endorsed by many leading AI researchers and organizations around the world and continue to influence the development of AI policy and practice.

Chapter 5

5–6 SOURCE CODE: WHAT THE HELL IS IT?

"Source code" is a list of commands used to create software, including AI systems. It is the set of instructions that tell computers what to do. However, "open-source" means that the source code is available for anyone to see and modify, while "closed-source" means that the source code is kept secret and not available for others to access or modify.

Open-source AI code can be valuable for fighting AI-driven psychological programming because it allows more people to see how the software works and potentially identify any harmful or manipulative tactics being used. Closed-source AI code is chosen over open-source code for various reasons, such as protecting intellectual property or maintaining a competitive advantage in the market.

5–7 OPEN AND CLOSED SOURCE CODE

Open-source code AI development fosters an environment for transparent AI systems and collaborative environments for AI research. "Open source" refers to a type of software or technology where the source code (the instructions that tell the technology what to do) are freely available to the public to view, modify, and distribute. This contrasts with closed-source code technology, where the source code is kept secret and only accessible to the company or individuals who created it.

Open-source code is valuable for fighting AI-driven psychological programming because it allows for greater transparency and collaboration in the development and implementation of AI technologies. When the code is open source, it can be reviewed and audited by experts and concerned individuals to ensure it is not being used to harm people. Additionally, open source allows for the development of ethical and responsible AI, as it can be collaboratively developed and evaluated by a larger and more diverse community.

Closed source AI code is frequently favored over open source code for a variety of reasons. One reason is companies that invest heavily in developing AI systems may wish to keep their technology secret from competitors. As a result, they use closed source code to safeguard their intellectual property. This protects their investment in the development of the technology and prevents competitors from accessing it.

Another advantage of closed source code is that it can be more easily commercialized. Companies that use closed source code can license their software to customers and generate income from their technology. This provides them with a way to monetize their AI technology and fund further research and development.

Finally, some argue that closed source code is more secure. As the source code is not available for attackers to scrutinize and find vulnerabilities, it may be more difficult for them to exploit any weaknesses in the system. This is particularly important for companies that use AI in sensitive industries, such as finance or healthcare, where security breaches could have severe consequences.

However, closed source code also has drawbacks. For example, it can limit innovation as developers cannot collaborate and build on existing code, and it can also limit transparency and accountability in AI systems. Additionally, it can lead to "vendor lock-in," where customers become dependent on a specific vendor for their AI solutions.

AI code can still remain proprietary even if it's open source to the developers even though it can be reviewed, modified, and distributed. A company or developer may release the source code for an AI program as open source but require anyone who uses it to give credit to the company or prohibit them from using it for commercial purposes.

Chapter 5

Therefore, the code is still proprietary, but it's just being shared in a more open and collaborative way.

Open-source and closed source AI systems should be required to be identified for the user. Then the user can decide whether they want to use a closed-source AI system that's more likely to be used for psychological manipulation. Open-source AI systems typically create better and more ethical AI systems. While both closed and open-source AI systems can be used for AI-driven psychological programming, closed-source AI systems are more likely to be used in such situations where individuals or organizations want to maintain control over their technology and limit others' access to it. However, this doesn't mean that all closed-source AI systems are only used for nefarious purposes, nor that all open-source AI systems are immune from unethical use.

> *It's critical for institutions to understand how the race*
> *between AI labs is accelerating the likelihood of catastrophe.*
> Tristan Harris | American Technology Ethicist
> Co-Founder of the Center for Humane Technology

5-8   THIRD-PARTY AUDITS – CHECKS AND BALANCES FOR AI

Third-party audits should be employed to assess AI systems for biases, vulnerabilities, ethical and national security concerns. A third-party audit is an evaluation of a company, organization, or process by an independent, unbiased third-party entity. The purpose of a third-party audit provides an objective assessment of whether the entity being audited is following established standards, regulations, and best practices.

In the context of AI-driven psychological programming, a third-party audit can be used to assess whether a company or organization is using AI in an ethical and responsible manner. The third-party auditor can review the AI system's design, implementation, and operation, as well as evaluate the system's impact on individuals and society. The auditor can also recommend improvements, report national security concerns or corrective actions to ensure that the AI system is aligned with ethical principles, the values of a nation, and the law.

5-9   MEDIA LITERACY AND JOURNALISTIC INTEGRITY

To better equip citizens with the necessary tools to critically evaluate the information they consume and recognize potential manipulation or misinformation resulting from AI-driven psychological programming, media literacy programs should be integrated into educational curriculums at all levels. For example, students should be trained to assess the reliability of news sources, identify deepfake videos, and discern disinformation campaigns.

Freedom-loving countries should develop public-private partnerships to bring together private companies, research institutions, and government agencies to develop best practices for regulating AI-driven psychological programming in order to deter national security threats. AI literacy programs, such as an AI for K-12 initiative, should be utilized to educate students about AI technology and its ethical considerations.

Encouraging the responsible use of AI in journalism is essential to ensuring the dissemination of accurate news and preventing the amplification of misinformation. This is especially important for young people who consume news on a regular basis. However, it has been observed that research conducted with AI tools can sometimes result in selective search results, leading to selective reporting by journalists. As young people grow into adults and become journalists themselves, this issue needs to be addressed. It is important to keep in mind the adage, "Garbage in—Garbage out" because as of now, AI tends to provide selective information, resulting in a finished

Chapter 5

journalistic product that is also selective. This, in turn, strengthens one perspective while erasing another. There have been instances where AI has been corrupted and used to promote cultural Marxist ideologies while giving the appearance of impartiality. It is crucial to remain vigilant and promote ethical AI practices in journalism to ensure the current and future integrity of fair and balanced news reporting rather than subtle PSYOP via selective information.

5-10   EXPORT RESTRICTIONS

Strengthening technology export controls can impede the proliferation of AI-driven psychological programming tools and technologies to nations or entities that may misuse them for malicious purposes. Technology export controls refer to regulations put in place by governments to restrict or limit the export of certain technologies or products to other countries, particularly those that are deemed sensitive or have military applications.

With regard to AI, technology export controls may be used to prevent the spread of AI-driven psychological programming tools and technologies to countries or entities that may use them for malicious purposes against freedom-loving countries, such as undermining the psychological stability of the citizenry of a target nation or manipulating public opinion for the political gain of adversaries.

These controls are important in the context of AI-driven psychological programming, because the technology has the potential to be used as a weapon against a country's citizens, particularly in the hands of hostile nations or organizations. By strengthening the restriction of the export of such technologies, governments can limit their availability to those who may use them for malicious purposes, ensuring they are only used for peaceful and ethical applications.

In 2022, the U.S. Government restricted Nvidia (the U.S.-based AI chipmaker) from exporting AI computer chips for high performance computing to foreign countries that included China and Russia. Oversight must increase to avoid the potential for third party straw sales to bad actors. National security requires the same level of scrutiny for AI chips as there is for depleted uranium that used to make nuclear weapons.

5-11   WHISTLEBLOWER PROTECTIONS AND AI ETHICS IN CORPORATE CULTURE

Reporting mechanisms with whistleblower protections can play a crucial role in stopping the use of foreign-born AI-driven psychological programming by encouraging individuals to report any unethical use of AI. By providing legal protection to whistleblowers, individuals who witness or suspect the misuse of AI technology can come forward without fear of retaliation. This can help uncover instances of AI-driven psychological programming being used to manipulate individuals and groups, spread false information, negatively impact elections, and compromise national security.

Furthermore, integration of AI ethics into corporate culture can also be instrumental in promoting responsible use of AI within organizations. By establishing ethical guidelines and principles for the development and use of AI technology, companies can ensure that their AI systems are not being used for unethical purposes such as manipulating public opinion or inciting violence for the purpose of assisting our nation's adversaries. This can help prevent the misuse of AI technology for psychological programming, as companies will be incentivized to prioritize these listed considerations in their development and deployment of AI systems.

The place we need to start is integration across agencies in the U.S. Government . . . we need to get some central coordination body going over white world information sharing . . . somebody has to be in charge of informa-

Chapter 5

tion. In the military parlance we talk about the levers of national power is the D.I.M.E., Diplomacy, Information, Military, Economic and there's others. There is a cabinet level secretary for all of those, except the "I". There is no cabinet level secretary for Information... I spent my whole life studying war; bombs and bullets and I'm telling you... I'm scared to death we are going to lose [to China] in the information space.

General David Stilwell, USAF (Ret.) | May 3, 2023, Testimony before the Subcommittee on State Department and USAID Management, International Operations, and Bilateral International Development: SUBCOMMITTEE HEARING | THE GLOBAL INFORMATION WARS: IS THE U.S. WINNING OR LOSING? *[Explanation for "White World Information Sharing" can be found in section 6–5, Session II]*

5-12   THE ROLE OF INDIVIDUAL STATES

A coalition of Governors must be formed immediately with the commitment of making their states more independent of the federal government by developing sustainably sourced in-state programs to ensure access to food, energy, and water. The formation of a coalition of Governors committed to making their states more independent of the federal government by developing sustainably sourced in-state programs can help protect people from the effects of AI-driven psychological programming by ensuring access to basic resources such as food, energy, and water. By developing these resources locally, the coalition can reduce reliance on external entities, including those that may use AI-driven psychological programming to manipulate the population or disrupt access to vital resources. This could also promote a sense of community and shared responsibility for the well-being of citizens, which could potentially counteract the isolation and division that can result from such programming. The development of sustainable local resources promotes resilience and protects against external threats, including those posed by AI-driven psychological programming.

The idea behind developing sustainably sourced in-state programs for food, energy, and water is to create greater independence and resilience at the state level. By reducing reliance on external sources for these vital resources, states can better protect their citizens from disruptions caused by factors such as manipulated disasters, cyber-attacks, or even foreign interference resulting in shortages caused by CCP control of goods and resources.

For example, if a state relies heavily on imports for its food supply and those imports are disrupted due to fifth generation warfare attacks by the CCP, the state could face food shortages and even famine. However, if the state had its own sustainable agriculture

Chapter 5

programs in place, it would be better equipped to provide for its citizens in such a scenario.

Similarly, ensuring access to sustainable sources of energy and water helps protect citizens from disruptions caused by such events that could knock out power grids or contaminate water supplies.

The goal of these in-state programs is to promote greater resilience and self-sufficiency, which will help protect citizens from the effects of AI-driven psychological programming and other fifth generation warfare attacks on the existing centralized infrastructure. Self-sufficiency removes factors that can be used to manipulate the citizenry.

5-13   WHEN THE USE OF FOREIGN-BORN AI-DRIVEN PSYCHOLOGICAL PROGRAMMING BECOMES AN ACT OF WAR

The use of foreign-born AI-driven psychological programming poses a significant threat to national security and the safety of citizens. Therefore, a comprehensive approach is necessary to effectively regulate it and protect the American people. If this technology causes significant harm, such as manipulation of elections, incitement of violence, or dissemination of propaganda to incite rebellion, or civil unrest, it should be considered an act of war. In such cases, the Department of Defense and the Department of State would have crucial responsibilities in responding to these acts of aggression.

While AI-driven psychological programming may seem like a new and enigmatic form of attack on the American people, it is important to recognize that we are at war now. Therefore, kinetic military force against adversaries conducting these attacks may be necessary to stop them from destroying our country. However, it is also important to prevent foreign adversaries from accessing the cognitive battlespace of our citizenry.

Failure to recognize this emerging operational environment and address the threats it poses could result in our demise. In short, the regulation of foreign-born AI-driven psychological programming is essential to national security, and swift action is necessary to prevent harm to our people and the death of our country. AI is more profitable than oil and it's the nuclear weapon of our time.

The great error of nearly all studies of war...
has been to consider war as an episode in foreign policies
when it is an act of interior politics.
Simone Weil | Philosopher and Political Activist

Chapter 5

Chapter 5
Homework Break

Please consider all the information presented so far, while seeking additional information and using your critical thinking skills to answer these questions. Write your answers on this page.

1. According to section 5-1, how long do we have to make ten years of progress?

2. According to section 5-9, why is strengthening technology export controls important?

3. Explain the importance of third-party audits?

4. In section 5–11, what is the role of the Coalition of Governors and why is it important?

Chapter 5

Chapter 6
Open-Source Intelligence:
OSINT for Civilians

Information is a source of learning.
But unless it is organized, processed,
and available to the right people
in a format for decision making,
it is a burden, not a benefit.
C. William Pollard | *The Soul of the Firm*

NOTE: According to the OSINT Foundation, OSINT is pronounced "OH-sint" (there is no "zee" or /z/ sound when pronouncing OSINT)

6–1   GRAB WHAT YOU CAN

The community of intelligence agencies, such as the Central Intelligence Agency (CIA) and the National Security Agency (NSA), uses OSINT to monitor foreign media and online sources for information about potential threats and to track the activities of foreign governments and organizations. This information is then used to inform U.S. national security and foreign policy decisions.

Another example is the United Kingdom's foreign intelligence agency, MI6. MI6 uses OSINT to gather information about foreign governments and organizations, as well as to track potential threats to UK national security. This involves monitoring social media and other online sources for information and analyzing it to gain insight into the activities and intentions of foreign entities. OSINT is used by nearly all governments and their respective intelligence agencies to gather information for national security and foreign policy purposes.

6-2   WHY CIVILIANS NEED OSINT

Open-Source Intelligence (OSINT) offers numerous benefits for civilians to empower themselves to make informed decisions and to enhance the personal safety and security of the citizenry. By accessing and analyzing a wide range of publicly available information resources on various subjects, such as politics, local events, consumer products, or personal interests, the civilian populace empowers themselves with a better understanding of specific topics to engage in meaningful non-polarizing discussions. For instance, understanding political stances during an election can help civilians vote more responsibly and equally be able to take their not-so-favorite podcaster to task to keep them honest.

OSINT also plays a crucial role in assessing potential threats and risks that might present themselves. By staying informed about crime rates, natural disasters, cybersecurity threats, geopolitics, online scams, and other hazards, individuals can take appropriate precautions to protect themselves, family members, and other important things. This awareness enables civilians to better protect their digital assets and personal information from potential risks.

OSINT empowers civilians through knowledge and access to diverse sources of information. This empowerment provides individuals with the tools and resources necessary to develop informed opinions, choices, and be proactive within communities.

By promoting critical thinking and informed discussions, OSINT helps the citizenry identify and debunk all forms of misinformation or disinformation, contributing to a more informed and engaged society. It also reduces individual susceptibility to manipulation and propaganda.

Chapter 6

6–3　　OSINT - IT'S WHAT THE COOL KIDS DO – DO IT

Being able to collect Open-Source Intelligence (OSINT) or "do OSINT," like the cool kids say, gives you power. Use the information that is everywhere: it's publicly available on the internet, in news media, and government databases. By learning about OSINT and how to effectively use it, citizens can reap several benefits.

One primary benefit of OSINT is the ability to personally and effectively fact-check information and verify claims made by individuals, organizations, and governments. In today's world where misinformation and fake news are prevalent, having access to accurate information is critical for making informed decisions. Ditch the rumors and social media chit-chat that is designed to provoke emotion and shut down your logical brain.

Open-Source Intelligence (OSINT) refers to the collection, analysis, and dissemination of publicly available information to support decision-making processes. The *U.S. Army Field Manual 2-22.9, Open-Source Intelligence (OSINT) (2006),* provides guidelines and procedures for the military OSINT process. OSINT can be used for various purposes, such as threat intelligence, competitive analysis, or research. Below is a step-by-step guide, with some basic resources to get you started on how to conduct Open-Source Intelligence:

STEP 1

Define Your Objectives: Clearly outline your goals and objectives for the OSINT process. Determine the specific information you need and the purpose for which it will be used. When conducting OSINT as a civilian, it is important to clearly outline your goals and objectives to ensure you gather relevant and actionable information. For example, if a civilian wants to understand the local government's stance on tax issues and their proposed policies, they should set specific goals and objectives to maintain focus.

The first goal might be to gain a comprehensive understanding of the local government's tax policies and initiatives, with objectives such as identifying key tax issues addressed by the local government, researching proposed policies, and understanding the government's track record in implementing previous tax initiatives.

The second goal could be to assess the impact of proposed taxes on the local community, with objectives like investigating potential benefits and drawbacks of the policies, evaluating the community's support or opposition to these policies, and identifying stakeholders, such as businesses, groups and organizations that may be affected by the policies. By defining clear goals and objectives, the civilian can maintain focus on the specific information needed and avoid getting off track.

This targeted approach helps ensure that the collected information is relevant, useful, and aids in achieving the desired understanding of the subject matter. The bottom line here is don't chase rabbits down every rabbit hole. Decide what you intend to do and follow a sensible path to the goal. If you have more than one goal, each goal requires its own separate clear path. Synthesis of more than one goal comes after the verification step listed below.

STEP 2

Identify Information Sources: Compile a list of publicly available sources that might contain relevant information. These sources can include websites, social media platforms, forums, blogs, news outlets, academic publications, government databases, and more. When identifying information sources for OSINT purposes, civilians can access a wide range of publicly available sources to gather relevant information. Maps and geospatial data from various sources offer geographic context.

Maps are widely overlooked and provide valuable information. Starting with a map search is generally a good idea. Websites, social media platforms, forums, blogs, news outlets, academic publications, and government databases give civilians access to explore public records such as property records, business registrations, and court documents. Looking at primary source documents typically provides information overlooked by the less thorough researchers and provides information that others won't have.

Video and audio sharing platforms like YouTube, GETTR, GAB, Rumble, and the numerous podcast directories available provide insightful content like interviews and presentations. Professional networks like LinkedIn and specialized forums like Reddit or Quora can connect civilians with experts or individuals with firsthand knowledge on specific topics. Information from non-governmental organizations (NGOs), company and organizational websites, as well as local newspapers and community publications, can also prove valuable. Always look at the comments in local news sources and there's often a few good nuggets. But be aware of bots.

Always find the path to the source documents. If you see someone reporting about a document and they don't provide the source document, don't be afraid to question their reporting. Reports and analyses from think tanks and research organizations can offer expert perspectives on various subjects. Online databases and libraries provide access to historical documents and scholarly articles. Data repositories and open-data platforms like data.gov and data.worldbank.org offer valuable datasets and statistics.

By exploring a diverse range of publicly available sources, civilians can obtain a comprehensive understanding of a subject and reduce the risk of misinformation or bias. We've provided a few online resources for you to get started. Find more on your own. The authors of Session II of this *Guide* have not been compensated by the resources listed below. Our intention is for the reader to get a sense of balance when looking for information.

What follows are four resources that may be of interest to conservatives. While data repositories and open-data platforms are typically non-partisan and provide neutral information, some resources may be favored by conservative-leaning users due to the content they provide or the organizations they are affiliated with.

> 1. **National Review – (www.nationalreview.com)** *National Review* is a conservative magazine and website that publish-

es news, opinions, and analysis on politics and government, including election-related topics. They often provide data-driven articles and commentaries, which can be of interest to conservative users.

2. **RealClearPolitics** – **(www.realclearpolitics.com)** RealClear-Politics is a popular website that provides political news, analysis, and polling data. It is known for its aggregation of polling data and election forecasts, which can be useful for those interested in tracking trends from a conservative perspective.

3. **The American Conservative** – **(www.theamericanconservative.com)** *The American Conservative* is a magazine and website that publishes news, analysis, and commentary from a conservative perspective. While not a data repository or open-data platform, it can provide insights and perspectives on electoral issues and policies that are relevant to conservatives.

4. **The Gateway Pundit** – **(www.thegatewaypundit.com)** The Gateway Pundit is a conservative news and opinion website

that covers various topics, including politics, culture, and current events. While not strictly an election data platform, it often reports on electoral events, policies, and issues from a conservative perspective. The website is known for its right-leaning reporting and remains a popular source for those seeking conservative viewpoints and commentary.

It's important to note that though the resources above may have a conservative-leaning editorial stance, the data and information they provide can still be valuable for understanding political trends.

Below are four resources that may be of interest to liberal leaning readers and researchers. While data repositories and open-data platforms are typically non-partisan and provide neutral information, some resources may be favored by liberal-leaning users due to the content they provide or the organizations they are affiliated with.

1. **The Center on Budget and Policy Priorities – (www.cbpp.org)** The Center on Budget and Policy Priorities is a public policy resource that provides research, analysis, and commentary on various policy issues. While not strictly an election data platform, it can offer insights and perspectives on electoral policies and issues from a liberal viewpoint.

Chapter 6

2. **The Nation** – (www.thenation.com) *The Nation i*s a progressive magazine and website that publishes news, opinions, and analysis on politics and government, including election-related topics. They often provide data-driven articles and commentaries, which can be of interest to liberal users.

3. **FiveThirtyEight** – (www.fivethirtyeight.com) FiveThirtyEight is a popular website that provides statistical analysis and data-driven journalism on politics, sports, and other topics. It is known for its aggregation of polling data and election forecasts, which can be useful for those interested in tracking trends from a liberal perspective.

4. **The American Prospect** – (www.prospect.org) *The American Prospect* is a magazine and website that publishes news, analysis, and commentary from a liberal perspective. While not a data repository or open-data platform, it can provide insights and perspectives on electoral issues and policies that are relevant to liberals.

It's important to note that though the resources above may have a liberal-leaning editorial stance, the data and information they provide can still be valuable for understanding political trends.

The following five think tanks make policy recommendations and are generally considered to lean conservative or have a Republican orientation. These organizations often provide research, analysis, and policy recommendations that align with conservative or Republican-leaning ideologies. Keep in mind that the degree of political leaning can vary across different think tanks and within specific research areas.

> **1. The Heritage Foundation – (www.heritage.org)** A prominent conservative think tank that focuses on limited government, free markets, and individual liberty. The Heritage Foundation advocates for conservative public policies based on free enterprise, limited government, individual freedom, and a strong national defense.

> **2. American Enterprise Institute (AEI) – (www.aei.org)** A public policy research institute dedicated to defending human dignity, expanding human potential, and building a freer and safer world. American Enterprise Institute (AEI) supports free markets, limited government, and a strong defense, and often

provides policy recommendations based on these principles.

3. **Cato Institute – (www.cato.org)** A libertarian think tank that promotes limited government, individual liberty, free markets, and peace. The Cato Institute provides policy recommendations based on these principles.

4. **Hoover Institution – (www.hoover.org)** Located at Stanford University, this public policy think tank focuses on economic policy, national security, and individual freedom. Hoover Institution focuses on individual, economic, and political freedom, private enterprise, and limited government. It may also provide policy recommendations in line with these principles.

5. **The Heartland Institute – (www.heartland.org)** This think tank focuses on free-market solutions to social and economic problems, with an emphasis on deregulation and limited government intervention. The Heartland Institute promotes free-market solutions to social and economic issues. It may also provide policy recommendations consistent with their perspective.

Chapter 6

The following five think tanks make policy recommendations and are generally considered to lean liberal or have a Democrat orientation. These organizations often provide research, analysis, and policy recommendations aligning with liberal or Democrat-leaning ideologies. Keep in mind that the degree of political leaning can vary across different think tanks and within specific research areas.

1. **Brookings Institution – (www.brookings.edu)** A prominent public policy organization that conducts research and analysis on various issues, with a focus on social welfare, economic development, and international affairs. Brookings Institution aims to maintain intellectual independence and is committed to open-minded, fact-based analysis, and it is often perceived as leaning liberal in its policy recommendations.

2. **Center for American Progress (CAP) – (www.americanprogress.org)** This progressive policy institute focuses on improving the lives of Americans through bold, progressive ideas and action. Center for American Progress (CAP) advocates for progressive ideas and policy recommendations on issues such

Chapter 6

as economic policy, social policy, and national security.

3. **Urban Institute – (www.urban.org)** This research organization focuses on economic and social policy issues, with an emphasis on social equity and inclusion. While the Urban Institute is committed to maintaining nonpartisanship and independence, it often leans liberal in its policy recommendations on issues such as social and economic policy.

4. **RAND Corporation – (www.rand.org)** This nonprofit, nonpartisan research organization focuses on a wide range of policy issues, including health, education, national security, and international affairs. RAND conducts research and analysis across a wide range of policy areas. While it is committed to nonpartisanship, it often leans left on policy recommendations based on its research findings.

5. **The Brennan Center for Justice – (www.brennancenter.org)** This research and advocacy organization focuses on issues concerning the law for which they make policy recommendations.

The following three resources don't make policy recommendations but are considered neutral between Republicans and Democrats.

1. The Pew Research Center – (www.pewresearch.org)
Considered a nonpartisan and impartial think tank, The Pew Research Center conducts public opinion polling, demographic research, content analysis, and other data-driven social science research. The organization does not take policy positions. Its research aima to providw unbiased information on social issues, public opinion, and demographic trends shaping the United States and the world.

Although no organization can be entirely free of bias, the Pew Research Center is widely respected for its commitment to rigorous methodology and maintaining a neutral stance in its research. It's the only think tank listed here that does not take policy positions.

2. The Epoch Times – (www.theepochtimes.com) *The Epoch Times,* a newspaper and a website, offers extensive coverage on a variety of topics, such as politics, business, world news, culture, and more. Known for providing ground-truth reporting that exposes the Chinese Communist Party (CCP), it is run by individuals who escaped persecution in China and who are pro-America.

3. Ballotpedia – (www.ballotpedia.org) *Ballotpedia* is a non-partisan online encyclopedia that covers American politics and elections. It provides comprehensive information on candidates, political parties, and election issues that you may find useful.

STEP 3

Select Tools and Techniques: Choose the appropriate OSINT tools and techniques based on your objectives and the type of data you search for. Tools can include search engines, data mining tools, social media monitoring platforms, web scrapers, reverse image searches, online forums and communities, network analysis tools, geolocation tools, and data visualization tools, among others. Take the time to research the OSINT applications for each of these tools. Some are complex and are subscription based while others are free and easy to use.

STEP 4

Data Collection: Use the selected tools and techniques as listed in STEP 3 to collect relevant data from your identified sources. This may involve keyword searches, monitoring specific social media accounts, or extracting data from websites.

STEP 5

Data Analysis: Organize, process, and analyze the collected data to extract useful insights. This involves techniques such as text analysis, sentiment analysis, pattern recognition, link analysis, and geospatial analysis. Organizing, processing, and analyzing collected data provides civilians with useful insights into various topics, such as understanding public opinion on a new city policy.

Text analysis analyzes local newspaper articles, blog posts, and social media posts, to identify frequently mentioned topics or keywords related to the policy. This helps civilians grasp the key aspects of the policy and the ongoing discussions.

Sentiment analysis examines public reactions on social media platforms, comments sections of local news websites, and online forums to determine the overall sentiment. This gives civilians a sense of how the community feels about the policy.

Pattern recognition identifies recurring themes, concerns, or arguments in the collected data, revealing underlying issues or popular opinions among community members.

Link analysis investigates relationships between key stakeholders, such as local politicians, community leaders, and advocacy groups, by examining their online interactions and shared content, allowing civilians to understand potential alliances or conflicts of interest related to the policy.

Geospatial analysis, on the other hand, maps public sentiment or policy-related incidents across different neighborhoods or areas within the city. This helps civilians identify geographical patterns and areas with higher levels of support or opposition to the policy, providing valuable context for understanding local dynamics and the issue at hand.

STEP 6

Verification: Validate the accuracy and reliability of the information you've gathered. Cross-check facts and data points with multiple sources and consider the credibility of the sources themselves. Verification is an essential step in ensuring the accuracy and reliability of the information gathered by civilians.

For example, when examining claims about the effectiveness of a proposed city infrastructure project, such as a new public transportation system, civilians can cross-check facts and data points with multiple sources. They can consult official government documents and press releases, review expert opinions from urban planners, engineers, and local community organizations, and compare similar infrastructure projects in other cities to understand the outcomes and lessons learned.

To evaluate the credibility of these sources, civilians should consider the expertise and qualifications of the authors, such as their professional background, education, and experience in the relevant field. They should also assess the objectivity and impartiality of the sources, being cautious of potential biases or conflicts of interest, such as financial ties to the project or strong political affiliations.

Chapter 6

Lastly, it's important to ensure the timeliness of the information, making certain that the data and opinions are up-to-date and relevant to the current context of the project. By cross-checking information from various sources and considering their credibility, civilians can verify the accuracy and reliability of the information they gather, leading to a more informed understanding of the topic at hand.

STEP 7

Synthesize and Report: Prepare yourself as if you are compiling your findings into a coherent and actionable report. Summarize key insights, highlight trends, and provide recommendations based on your analysis. The information may only be for you but you should be able to articulate your findings to a group as well.

STEP 8

Disseminate Information: Share your findings with others, such as team members or decision-makers if you are part of an organization or group of people working together. Present the information in a clear and concise manner, and tailor the presentation to your audience's needs.

Perhaps only your family and friends will be privileged enough to enjoy your findings or just maybe, you'll be able to keep your favorite podcaster, media personality, Twitter rival, or politician a little more honest.

STEP 9

Review and Update: Continuously monitor your information sources and update your analysis as new data becomes available. This will help you stay current and ensure that your intelligence remains relevant and accurate.

STEP 10

Maintain Operational Security: Protect your identity and the privacy of your research subjects. Use tools like VPNs, secure browsers, and anonymizing services to conduct your research safely and responsibly.

When maintaining operational security while conducting OSINT research, there are several tools and techniques that helps protect your identity and the privacy of your research subjects. Utilize VPNs such as ProtonVPN, TunnelBear, or Windscribe to encrypt your internet connection and mask your IP address.

Browse securely with privacy-focused browsers like Tor Browser, Brave, or Firefox, and consider using extensions such as HTTPS Everywhere, Privacy Badger, and uBlock Origin. Access websites anonymously with services like Tor or I2P and use disposable email services like Mailinator, 10 Minute Mail, or Guerrilla Mail when signing up for online services.

Communicate securely using encrypted messaging apps like Signal, Wire, or Wickr and store research files securely on encrypted cloud storage platforms like Tresorit, Mega, or Sync. Run virtual machines (VM) such as VirtualBox, VMware, or Qubes OS for an isolated research environment, and encrypt sensitive data with tools like VeraCrypt or AxCrypt.

Use privacy-focused search engines like Brave and adjust your social media privacy settings to limit the visibility of your personal information. Employing these tools and techniques helps ensure that your OSINT research is conducted safely and responsibly.

6-4   TRACK PROPAGANDA / DISINFORMATION CAMPAIGNS

OSINT can be used to track propaganda campaigns conducted by governments or other organizations. By monitoring social media and other online sources, individuals can identify patterns of misinformation and disinformation, and determine the sources and motives behind these campaigns.

During the Cold War, the Soviet government conducted a widespread propaganda campaign aimed at promoting the ideals of communism and discrediting the West. In response, the Western governments and their allies launched their own anti-Soviet propaganda campaign.

Using OSINT techniques, individuals and organizations were able to track and analyze the propaganda campaigns of both the Soviet and Western governments. They monitored the content of propaganda materials, such as newspapers, posters, and films, and compared it to independent sources of information to determine the accuracy and objectivity of the information being presented. This allowed them to identify patterns of misinformation and disinformation and to determine the motives behind these propaganda campaigns.

Governments routinely engage in disinformation campaigns, spreading false information to manipulate public opinion or to distract from important issues. By using OSINT, citizens can fact-check this information and determine the accuracy of the information being presented to them. For example, they can use online forums and multiple social media platforms to see what other citizens are saying about the information being released, or they can use independent sources to verify the accuracy of the information being presented by the government.

In 2018, the United Kingdom government claimed that the Russian government was behind the poisoning of former Russian spy Sergei Skripal and his daughter Yulia in Salisbury, England. Independent analysts were able to fact-check the information being presented by the government and to determine the accuracy of the claims.

They monitored government statements and intelligence reports, compared them to independent sources, and used open-source tools to analyze images and other data. This led to increased public skepticism about the evidence presented by the government and helped to promote greater transparency and accountability in government.

6-5   WHITE – GRAY – BLACK

Though all propaganda is meant to relay a message to a target audience, it doesn't mean all propaganda is false information. White, gray, and black propaganda are types of propaganda distinguished by their source, transparency, and content. Each has a different level of credibility, deception, and intent. Here's a comparison and contrast between the three types:

WHITE PROPAGANDA

- **Source:** White propaganda originates from an acknowledged and clearly identified source.

- **Transparency:** The information presented is largely accurate and truthful, although it may be selectively presented or biased to support the originator's objectives.

- **Intent:** White propaganda aims to influence public opinion, typically in a positive manner, and promotes the originator's perspective or agenda. Examples include government press releases, official statements, and public diplomacy materials.

GRAY PROPAGANDA

- **Source:** Gray propaganda has an ambiguous or unclear source, making it difficult to trace back to its origin.

- **Transparency:** The information provided may contain a mix of truth, half-truths, and falsehoods, making it challenging to verify the accuracy of the content.

- **Intent:** Gray propaganda seeks to create confusion, uncertainty, or doubt about a particular issue or situation. It is used to manipulate public opinion by obscuring the true intent or agenda of the propagandist. Examples may include online blogs, anonymous social media accounts, or front organizations that disseminate information on behalf of a hidden entity.

BLACK PROPAGANDA

- **Source:** Black propaganda is intentionally attributed to a false source or disguised as coming from an enemy or neutral party.

- **Transparency:** The content is deliberately misleading, deceptive, or fabricated, with the intent to deceive the audience and create a false impression.

- **Intent:** Black propaganda aims to discredit, undermine, or harm the reputation of an individual, group, or nation by spreading false information, rumors, or lies. Examples include forged documents, fake news stories, or fabricated social media accounts that falsely represent the opposition.

White propaganda is the most transparent and truthful, originating from a known source and focusing on promoting a particular perspective. Gray propaganda is less transparent, with unclear sources and a mix of truth and falsehoods to sow confusion. However, some gray propaganda is more truthful than others and shouldn't immediately be discredited in instances when the originator must maintain their anonymity to avoid retribution. In these cases, OSINT and watching to see the source's credibility increase or decrease over time is especially important. Black propaganda is the most deceptive, disguising its origin and spreading false information to discredit or harm a target. By using OSINT tools and techniques you'll be able to identify the type of propaganda you are seeing.

Chapter 6

TYPES OF PROPAGANDA

 WHITE   **GRAY**   **BLACK**

HIGH ⟵ **SOURCE TRANSPARENCY** ⟶ LOW

DIAGRAM 6-5
WHITE - GRAY - BLACK

The Citizen's Guide to Fifth Generation Warfare
Session II

6-6   VERIFY OFFICIAL STATEMENTS

OSINT can be used to verify official statements made by governments and other organizations. By cross-referencing these statements with other sources of information, individuals can determine
the accuracy and completeness of the information being presented.
Often statements are accurate but incomplete and selective to make
individuals appear to say things they haven't.

Other times, official statements are false and used for manipulative
purposes. In 1964, the United States government claimed that the
North Vietnamese government had attacked two U.S. Navy destroy-
ers in the Gulf of Tonkin. This event was used to justify increased U.S.
military involvement in the Vietnam War. Through the use of OSINT
techniques, journalists, researchers, and independent analysts were
able to verify the official statements made by the government and to
determine the accuracy of the claims.

They cross-referenced the statements with other sources of information, including communication intercepts, ship logs, and eyewit-
ness accounts. This led to increased public skepticism about the
justification for the war and helped to promote greater transparency
and accountability in government.

You're not supposed to be
so blind with patriotism that
you can't face reality.
Wrong is wrong
no matter who does it
or who says it.
Malcolm X | Assassinated Civil Rights Leader

6-7   MONITOR MEDIA BIAS

OSINT can be used to monitor media bias, particularly in countries where freedom of the press is restricted. By tracking media coverage and comparing it to independent sources of information, individuals can determine the accuracy and objectivity of the information being presented by the government and other media outlets.

In China, the CCP heavily censors the media and restricts access to information. However, through the use of OSINT techniques, Chinese citizens have been able to monitor media bias and to access information that is being suppressed by the government.

For example, they have used circumvention tools, such as VPNs, to access foreign news outlets, and have used social media platforms, such as Weibo and WeChat, to share information and to mobilize against censorship and help the citizenry make informed decisions.

6–8   INVESTIGATE HUMAN RIGHTS ABUSE

OSINT can be used to investigate human rights abuses committed by governments or other organizations. By gathering and analyzing information from multiple sources, individuals can build a case for action and bring attention to human rights abuses that might otherwise go unnoticed.

Governments and human rights organizations use OSINT to investigate human rights abuses around the world. By gathering and analyzing information from various sources, they build a comprehensive understanding of the situation and identify potential human rights abuses. For example, the United Nations Office of the High Commissioner for Human Rights uses OSINT to monitor and document human rights abuses in conflict zones and other areas of concern.

Additionally, non-government organizations such as Human Rights Watch also use OSINT to gather evidence of human rights abuses and to advocate for action to address the situation. By utilizing OSINT, these organizations bring attention to human rights abuses and promote accountability for those responsible.

6–9   MISLEADING INFORMATION DURING A CRISIS

In times of a crisis, such as a natural disaster or a pandemic, governments may release information that is inaccurate or misleading. By using OSINT techniques, citizens can fact-check this information and determine the accuracy of the information being presented to them. For example, they can use search engines to find credible news sources and trusted independent fact-checkers to verify the accuracy of the information being released by the government.

6–10   IDENTIFY THREATS AND INCREASE SAFETY

OSINT can also be used to gather information about potential threats and to assess the safety of a given situation. For example, if a person is traveling to a new location, they can use OSINT to gather information about the local area and to identify any potential risks. In addition to personal safety, OSINT can be used for research and investigation purposes, such as conducting background checks on individuals or organizations. It can also be used to gather information about a wide range of topics, including current events, history, and culture, which can help to increase awareness and understanding of the world around us. If you are traveling to a new location, OSINT can be used to gather information about the local area, identify potential risks or allies, and promote informed decision-making.

6-11   BETTER UNDERSTAND YOUR SITUATION

By gathering and verifying information from multiple sources, individuals can make more informed decisions about important issues, such as investments, political decisions, and personal safety. OSINT can also be used to contextualize news events and to understand the facts behind the headlines, which can help to promote a more informed understanding of the world and to reduce the spread of misinformation. Furthermore, by learning about OSINT, individuals can better understand the information that is publicly available about them and can take steps to protect their privacy online. This can include removing personal information from public websites, adjusting privacy settings on social media accounts, and being mindful of what information is shared online.

Chapter 6

6-12   BETTER UNDERSTAND THE NEWS

OSINT can be used to contextualize news events and to understand the facts behind the headlines. This can help to promote a more informed understanding of the world and to reduce the spread of misinformation. OSINT can be used to verify information and to fact-check claims made by individuals, organizations, and governments. In a time where misinformation and fake news is prevalent, having the ability to access and verify information can be critical for making informed decisions.

6-13   IMPROVED CRITICAL THINKING SKILLS

By gathering information from multiple sources and verifying it through OSINT techniques, individuals can develop their critical thinking skills and become more discerning consumers of information. OSINT can be used to gather information about a wide range of topics, including current events, history, and culture. This can help to increase awareness and understanding of the world around us and to promote informed decision-making.

6-14   THE DO'S AND DON'TS OF OSINT FOR CIVILIANS

When conducting Open-Source Intelligence (OSINT), follow best practices and avoid common pitfalls. Consider the following do's and don'ts.

DO'S

1. Define Clear Objectives: A person researching local schools to choose the best one for their child might have objectives like comparing academic performance, extracurricular activities, and school safety records.

2. Use a Variety of Sources: A citizen researching a proposed city development project could consult news articles, city council meeting minutes, local forums, and the project's official website to get a comprehensive understanding.

3. Verify Information: When reading online reviews for a local restaurant, a person should check multiple review websites, such as Yelp, Google Reviews, and TripAdvisor, to get a more accurate understanding of the restaurant's quality.

4. Stay Organized: A person planning a vacation might create a spreadsheet or use a travel planning app to keep track of hotel options, tourist attractions, and transportation details.

5. Maintain Operational Security: When researching sensitive topics online, a citizen might use a VPN or a privacy-focused browser like Firefox or Brave to protect their privacy.

6. Respect Privacy: A person investigating a neighborhood dispute should avoid sharing personal information about the involved parties, such as their names or addresses, without their consent.

7. Stay Up to Date with Tools and Techniques: A citizen researching historical records for genealogy purposes could follow genealogy blogs or subscribe to newsletters to learn about new databases and research tools.

8. Collaborate with Others: A person seeking recommendations for a local contractor might ask friends, neighbors, or online community groups for their experiences and insights.

9. Be Patient and Persistent: A citizen researching a complex issue like local zoning laws might need to spend time reading multiple resources, contacting local officials, and attending public meetings to gain a thorough understanding.

10. Document Your Methodology: A person conducting research on local air quality could keep a record of the websites, databases, and tools they used, making it easier for others to understand and replicate their findings.

DON'TS

1. Don't Rely Solely on a Single Source: When researching local political candidates, a citizen should not rely solely on the candidates' campaign materials but also consult independent analyses, news articles, and public records.

2. Don't Ignore Context: A person reading a news article about a controversial community issue should consider the broader social, economic, and political context to better understand the situation.

3. Don't Forget to Assess Source Credibility: A citizen researching a health-related topic should prioritize information from reputable sources, such as government health agencies, medical journals, or well-regarded news outlets.

4. Don't Overlook Local or Niche Sources: A person researching the history of their town should consult local archives, historical societies, and community forums for unique insights not available from mainstream sources.

5. Don't Jump to Conclusions: A citizen should avoid forming an opinion about an issue based on a single social media post or news article without considering other perspectives and evidence.

6. Don't Neglect to Update Your Research: A person monitoring the progress of a local construction project should regularly check for updates from official sources and local news outlets as the project develops.

7. Don't Violate Legal or Ethical Boundaries: A citizen should not use deceptive tactics, like creating fake social media accounts, to gather information about others or access private information without permission.

8. Don't Forget About Data Security: A person storing sensitive personal information, such as financial or medical records, should use encryption and secure storage solutions to protect their data.

9. Don't Ignore Your Biases: A citizen researching a controversial community issue should be aware of their own biases and strive to approach the research objectively, considering multiple perspectives and weighing the evidence fairly.

10. Don't Underestimate the Importance of Presentation: If called to, be able to present your findings in a clear, concise, and engaging manner to ensure your audience understands and values your research. A person presenting their findings on a local environmental issue at a community meeting should use clear language, visual aids, and concise summaries to ensure that fellow community members can easily understand and engage with the information.

ADMIN NOTE: Special thanks to Patriot Mountain LLC of Clarksville, Tennessee, for helping to compile and for verifying the information in this chapter.

Chapter 6

Chapter 6
Homework Break

Please consider all the information presented so far, while seeking additional information and using your critical thinking skills to answer these questions. Write your answers on this page.

1. What is the value of OSINT?

2. Explain the major differences between white, gray, and black propaganda?

3. How many steps are in the OSINT process and what are they?

4. What is the 5th Don't?

Chapter 6

If you have
The Citizen's Guide to Fifth Generation Warfare
Session 1

. . . before reading Chapter 7,
please refer to the following sections.

Section 1–8
Section 9–6
Section 9–7

Chapter 7
Human Intelligence:
HUMINT for Civilians

For the loser now will be later to win,
for the times they are a-changin'.
Bob Dylan | "The Times They Are A-Changin'"

7-1 HUMINT

According to the U.S. Department of Defense's (DoD) *Dictionary of Military and Associated Terms (Joint Publication 1–02)*, defines HUMINT as "a category of intelligence derived from information collected and provided by human sources." In the military context, HUMINT often involves the gathering of intelligence through interpersonal interactions, such as interviews, interrogations, or direct observation. This information is collected by trained HUMINT collectors and can be a valuable source of intelligence for military decision-making and operations. These types of activities are conducted by highly trained people who have an extensive network to support them. You don't have the skills or support network needed for true intelligence collection.

However, as a civilian the basic concepts of HUMINT and a few pointers can provide you with first-hand information that can be used to gain valuable insights into various situations and events. This information can be obtained through direct conversations, interviews, observations, and other interactions with individuals who have direct knowledge of a particular situation or event.

7-2   NOTHING BEATS AN INTERVIEW - FLIRTABLITY MATTERS

All the examples used when discussing OSINT are augmented by the human factor in the Physical Domain *[ref: Session I 5GW Sections 9-6, 9-7]* and are not located on digital platforms. On some level the use of Human Intelligence (HUMINT) augments all OSINT. HUMINT is intelligence gathered by people from people. It involves the collection of information through human sources, such as spies, agents, or other individuals with access to the information being sought. For our purposes, we'll exclude the work done by spies and agents and focus on what is applicable to your survival. HUMINT is often used by intelligence agencies to gather information about foreign governments, military capabilities, and other sensitive information. The information gathered through HUMINT should be compared to OSINT you've collected. Using them together and the use of your critical thinking skills will be much more effective than self-radicalization provided by venting on social media. Your "venting" is how AI consumes human characteristics and learns how to manipulate the human race, so vent selectively. If you've ever flirted with someone who you wanted to return your affections, you can collect Human Intelligence.

7-3   USE WHAT YOU HAVE TO FIND PEOPLE WILLING TO TALK

First, you must find a person who knows what you need information about and then convince them to talk with you, but it's an opportunity to flip the script by using tech against itself for the purposes of good. We don't need to rely on a news source to tell us what's happening. Learn for yourself by leveraging what's available to get firsthand information.

If there's a news report about an incident in a specific area of the country, find people just like you who want to tell others what's happening. A savvy person can figure out how to negotiate with an UBER driver that's local to an area of interest to take video and explain what they see for a few bucks sent via your favorite payment transfer system. The same can be done with an online search for a local business near the area of interest. Locate a business, and a savvy person can probably find a person to talk to and ask questions.

Look at a Twitter post from an official source about the event and identify someone close to the area and send them a direct message, but only use a person seen on a thread with an official press release and don't use a thread based on a popular comment about the situation. Many news articles have a comment section, get your game on, and meet a new friend that made a comment and interests you. The key to selecting people from online news sources is making sure the news source is a local news source rather than a national or international news source.

7-4   NETWORKS OF PEOPLE

A hashtag is a network of people aligned with a topic. If you want to locate a person to talk to in Smithville, Ohio, and ask about an alleged uprising, locate a hashtag regarding that topic, perhaps

#PEACEFORSMITHVILLE. Look through the list of comments associated with the #PEACEFORSMITHVILLE hashtag and find a person you are basically personality-matched with.

If you are a 20-year-old male who likes poetry, find a commenter with similar interest. Keep it simple. Having common interests will make it easier to communicate and be relatable to each other. Don't contact just one person, chop it up with a few people. The people you want to respond to will most likely look over your profile to judge you and decide whether or not to respond.

If your profile is full of Marine Corps-related veteran topics, find someone you can evaluate as a person that will relate to you on a human level when they see your profile. Also, there might be times you mix it up and try to locate someone who's not the same as you to get a wider opinion. We highly suggest you have discussions with people not like you, because your neighbor is not your enemy.

7-5   ABC – ALWAYS BE COOL

Reaching out to people, whether an UBER driver, employee of a local business, commenter on social media, or someone you located in the comment section of a local newspaper or hashtag requires an element of levelheaded communication. Avoid loaded language of your own, and above all be likable and slightly ingratiating. Don't be fake. Be you. This is why you select someone you have personality matched yourself with, otherwise you won't speak each other's language. If you are contacting someone you are not personality matched with, explain that in the beginning and explain why you're trying to reach them.

If a paratrooper is trying to reach a fellow U.S. Army Paratrooper veteran, the communication might look like – "Hey bro . . . what's shakin'? I saw your comment on that hashtag and you got me thinking, ALL THE WAY! Is the shit going on like they say it is on the news?"

And if a grunt Marine veteran is trying to reach a professor of philosophy, the communication might look like this: "I respect what you said, Ma'am. Your comment on that hashtag really got me thinking. Thanks for being so honest and real with the truth. I realize on the surface we don't appear to have a lot in common, but may I ask you a serious question?"

Ask the person with whom you're personality matched a simple question in the first contact. With the person you aren't personality matched with, go a little slower: ingratiate them and ask if it's okay to ask a question. Stay cool, be likable and no diatribes about what you already think. You are a nice person who cares about people. Just do that: nothing more. If after three exchanges you haven't found a way to exchange a phone number, have a friendly text conversation or phone call, thank them, ingratiate them again, and step away. Otherwise, get close, respectfully ask what you want and let them know they can ask what they want as well. No pressure. Be your authentic self. Be likable.

7-6   EFFECTIVENESS

During the war in Iraq, a target audience *[ref: Session I 5GW Section 1-8]* for Sgt. Cutler's PSYOP Team was the children of Sadr City in Baghdad. By 2019 they had grown to be young adults, and in October 2019, the young people of Iraq led a non-violent revolution in Iraq, demanding equal rights, the rule of law, fair elections, and the removal of the Iranian-backed members of their government.

Boone Cutler used these techniques listed in Session II of *The Guide* to locate and connect with a person inside the Iraqi government who was empathetic to the desires of the young people. He was also a member of the Mehdi Militia whom Boone fought in Iraq. The connection was made through the hashtag #SAVETHEIRAQIPEOPLE. These techniques work and are usable by people worldwide who are looking to get ground-truth information and for building networks of likeminded people.

7-7   THE DO'S AND DON'TS OF HUMINT FOR CIVILIANS

DO'S

1. Obey the Law: Respect all laws and regulations during information collection. Ignorance of the law is no excuse. Do your due diligence.

2. Establish Rapport: Build trust with your source by being polite, respectful, and attentive.

3. Be Honest: Avoid misrepresenting yourself or your intentions. If they aren't interested in talking to you when you're honest, find someone who will.

4. Maintain Confidentiality: Protect the privacy of your sources and their information.

5. Practice Active Listening: Pay attention, ask open-ended questions, and confirm your understanding.

6. Verify Information: Cross-check data with other sources for accuracy and reliability.

7. Stay Aware: Maintain situational awareness and assess potential risks.

8. Document Your Findings: Keep detailed notes of your conversations for future reference.

9. Assess Source Credibility: Consider the reliability and motives of your source.

10. Be Patient: Allow time for your sources to open up and share information willingly.

DON'TS

1. Don't Engage with Minors, the Mentally Ill, or the Cognitively Impaired: These people are off-limits.

2. Don't Break the Law: Engaging in illegal activities puts your safety and your source's safety at risk. Ignorance of the law is no excuse: do your due diligence.

Chapter 7

3. Don't Forget Physical Security: Talk on the phone, online, through video conference or on FaceTime. It's more efficient and safer. Never meet a private person in-person and never tell people your location. If they can't respect this rule, find someone who will. Only be willing to meet public figures such as media contacts or politicians in public, professional settings, and never meet alone. Never privately and never alone.

4. Don't Pressure Your Source: Coercive tactics and unrealistic promises can lead to unreliable information.

5. Don't Disclose Sources: Protect the identity of your sources, especially when sharing sensitive information.

6. Don't Take Risks: Trust your gut and disengage from situations that feel unsafe. Do OSINT beforehand to assess risks and avoid them. You're an untrained civilian with no support system: don't forget it.

7. Don't Monopolize Conversations: Allow your source to speak freely and share their thoughts.

8. Don't Rely on a Single Source: Diversify your sources to reduce the risk of misinformation.

9. Don't Disregard Cultural Differences: Be sensitive to cultural norms and communication styles.

10. Don't Forget Operational Security: Use tools like VPNs, burner phones, dummy email accounts, and secure browsers to protect your identity and privacy.

7-8   BE LEGAL, BE MORAL, BE ETHICAL

In addition to privacy, learning about OSINT and HUMINT can also improve critical thinking skills and increase employability in fields such as journalism, law enforcement, intelligence analysis as well as build a smarter and more informed citizenry that's not tricked by Artificial Intelligence (AI) techniques. However, it is important to consider ethical considerations and to respect the privacy of individuals when conducting OSINT and HUMINT. You must ensure that any information obtained and used is obtained legally, morally, and ethically.

It is also important to understand that not all information found through OSINT is accurate or reliable and to always verify information through multiple means to ensure its accuracy. HUMINT is a good way to augment your OSINT game.

Chapter 7

Chapter 7
Homework Break

Please consider all the information presented so far, while seeking additional information and using your critical thinking skills to answer these questions. Write your answers on this page.

1. According to section 7-1, what don't you have?

2. According to section 7-3, what can a savvy person do?

3. What is the 1st Do?

4. What's the 1st Don't?

5. Can you use the information in Chapter 7 to help fact-check news reports?

Chapter 7

Chapter 8
Cultivating Propaganda to Use Against Them

In the midst of chaos,
there is also opportunity.

Sun Tzu | *The Art of War*

8-1   IDENTIFYING PROPAGANDA

OSINT can be used to identify and analyze propaganda, including visual and audio propaganda, by governments, intelligence agencies, and a well-informed citizenry. This information can help better understand the motivations and goals of the organizations behind the propaganda, which can be useful in developing counter-propaganda strategies.

For example, the government of a country may use OSINT to monitor and analyze propaganda spread by a foreign state to determine the motivations behind it and to develop a response. Another example could be a well-informed citizenry using OSINT to analyze propaganda spread by extremist organizations, to better understand their ideologies and tactics. By gathering and analyzing information from multiple sources, the government and intelligence agencies can gain a comprehensive understanding of propaganda and its impact, which can help to inform their response.

One current example of the use of OSINT to identify and analyze propaganda is the tracking of disinformation campaigns related to elections. In recent years, there have been numerous instances of foreign actors using social media and other online platforms to spread false information and manipulate public opinion in an effort to interfere with the electoral process. OSINT can be used to track the spread of this disinformation, to identify the sources behind it, and to assess its impact on public opinion.

By using a combination of tools and techniques, including data mining, network analysis, and sentiment analysis, researchers and investigators can build a comprehensive understanding of the disinformation landscape and develop strategies for countering it.

Chapter 8

8-2   SCAME - USING OSINT AND HUMINT FOR PROPAGANDA ANALYSIS

Analyzing propaganda is crucial for several reasons. First, it helps identify AI-driven psychological programming that comes from misinformation and disinformation, as propaganda often involves spreading false or misleading information. Analyzing it helps to debunk these falsehoods, preventing further dissemination, and reducing their impact on public opinion.

Second, understanding the intentions of the propagandist is essential. By analyzing propaganda, it's possible to gain insights into the objectives and goals of those who create and disseminate it, which can inform responses and strategies to counteract the propaganda and mitigate its effects.

Third, analyzing propaganda uncovers manipulation and persuasion techniques often used to influence the audience. This makes it easier for individuals to recognize and resist such tactics in the future. Lastly, analyzing propaganda contributes to improved media literacy by enabling individuals to think critically about the information they consume. This skill is vital in today's information-rich environment, where discerning reliable sources from biased or manipulative ones is essential.

Basic OSINT and HUMINT can be used to perform the SCAME technique of analyzing propaganda. Anything is better than knowing nothing, so avoid "forcing" information into this format if you do not know the actual information. Often, the true information appears after the propaganda has been analyzed or after other forms of intelligence data have been revealed. SCAME stands for Source, Content, Audience, Media and Effects and this chapter is solely dedicated to using the SCAME process for analyzing propaganda. The following is the SCAME process taken from the U.S. Army Field Manual 3–05.302 that's been put into civilian terms:

SOURCE

A source is the individual, organization, or government that sponsors and disseminates the propaganda. Source analysis should consider all of the various players involved in the design, development, and dissemination of the propaganda or information. Correct identification of the various sources behind a particular item of propaganda can assist in providing a clearer picture of the creator's capabilities and intent. The source may also be classified as white, gray, or black, if known. The following are types of sources:

1. **Actor.** An actor may be a true "actor" in the film or stage sense, or an actor may be the individual, social media influencer, animal, or representative the propaganda author/creator has selected to use to convey the propaganda message. In the instance of AI Driven psychological programming, the actor may simply be a person who is being promoted without previous intention or coordination simply because an AI system has identified them as useful.

2. **Authority.** Authority is the author/creator's means to establish credibility in the eyes of the intended Target Audience (TA). Authority can be manifested by means of individuals, symbols, slogans, or representations of items that resonate with the TA. An example is the use of the presidential seal on written documents produced in the U.S. Government. Another example is the Iraqi Minister of Information during Operation IRAQI FREEDOM. While the Iraqi Minister of Information's inaccurate statements had minimal impact on Western audiences, his position as a member of the Iraqi government did establish his authority to the Iraqi people. Always determine what the author/creator is using to give their propaganda authority so their

message of product might appear legitimate and credible.

3. Author/Creator. The author/creator is the individual or group who created or wrote the message or propaganda. The author/creator might be readily identifiable in many media forums when the propaganda is disseminated or in the propaganda itself. In addition to the individual authors, you should attempt to identify the production location where the propaganda was created or developed.

Try to identify who disseminated the propaganda. Sometimes, the dissemination means is obvious, as in the retransmission of a TV product via terrestrial retransmission sites, the internet, and print media. In many cases, you'll identify the dissemination source by applying other known facts about events relative to the situation or information that's being disseminated.

Potential dissemination sources include:

1. Government agencies
2. Police
3. Political parties
4. Politicians
5. Mass media
6. Military organizations

Chapter 8

7. Hired personnel
8. Volunteers
9. Social Media influencers
10. "Anonymous" entities
11. Podcasters
12. International media
13. Underground networks
14. Extremist groups

CONTENT

Analysis reveals what the propaganda message says and what is trying to be achieved regarding the TA. This analysis can also reveal the source's intent, motives, and goals. Content analysis reveals the meaning of the message, the reason the message was disseminated, the intended purpose or objective, and the manner in which the message was presented to the TA.

Analyze the content of propaganda by evaluating:

1. Objectives
2. Lines of persuasion used (i.e., stressing legitimacy of a specific political ideology)
3. Morale

4.   Involuntary information
5.   Biographic information
6.   Economic data
7.   Propaganda inconsistencies (i.e., if the TA is American citizens, it's inconsistent to use a line of persuasion directed at issues concerning Australian citizens)
8.   Geographic information
9.   Intentions

AUDIENCE

In this aspect of propaganda analysis, attempt to determine which TAs are being reached by the propaganda and which TAs were specifically selected by the author/creator. By viewing the TA via propaganda, you may become more aware of lines of persuasion and symbols that are more effective than others. The symbols used and stressed talking points, or specific language used help identify the group or individuals being targeted. This aspect of propaganda is critical, as it will, to a large part, determine which TA will be targeted for a potential counterpropaganda campaign.

The symbols, slogans, talking points, language, etc. are often the same for propaganda and counterpropaganda campaigns for the same TA: only the spin is different. It's the push and pull battle of propaganda. Audience analysis must be conducted in concert with content analysis, as content analysis will discover what behavior or attitude the author/creator seeks in the TA.

Audience analysis identifies four major classifications of Target Audiences (TA):

1. **Apparent.** Upon first observation, the propaganda appears to be intended for the apparent TA. The audience may or may not be the real intended or final targets of the propaganda. The author/creator may have selected the apparent TA deliberately or may simply be trying to deceive you. Closer examination and analysis may reveal a true TA beneath the obvious one.

2. **Ultimate.** The ultimate TAs are those audiences for whom the author/creator intended the message to get to, or those targets in which the author/creator desires a change of behavior or attitude. If the ultimate TA are university students, the intermediate TA could be the university professors and the unintended TA might be a mother of a university student who saw the propaganda their child brought home on spring break.

3. **Intermediate.** The author/creator uses the intermediate TA to assist in getting the message across to the ultimate TA. The intermediate audience may or may not be part of the ultimate TA. A media personality spreading the propaganda might be the intermediate TA.

4. **Unintended.** The unintended TAs are those audiences for whom the propaganda was not intended, but nonetheless received it.

The establishment of a CCP website in English represents a viable attempt to harness a worldwide dissemination tool. Further examination of the website reveals themes targeting Marxists as the ultimate TA.

The use of English as a language could be an attempt to use a common, worldwide language to reach Marxists around the world who may not speak Chinese. Western (sympathetic) Marxists are an additional potential TA. Another TA may be the English-speaking people in China, though such a small TA seems hardly worth the effort although they might be positioned as the apparent audience based on the content. Propaganda analysis involves the exploration of all possible TAs targeted by the author/creator. Look for all affected TAs within each of the four major audience classifications: Apparent, Ultimate, Intermediate, and Unintended. Each has their own perception and reason they were selected.

MEDIA

This aspect of propaganda analysis determines why a particular medium (type of media) was selected, what media capabilities the author/creator has, and how consistent the message was across a variety of media. Propaganda can be disseminated via visual, audio, and audiovisual means. Propaganda transmission modes may also be overt or covert.

Disseminated propaganda can show some weaknesses of the author/creator. Propaganda printed on inferior grades of paper may indicate supply shortages or a small-time operation. Weak broadcast signals, interrupted programs, poor production techniques, and a shortage of broadcast platforms may also indicate a lack of support or funding of the author/creator. Don't evaluate the effectiveness of the propaganda based only on production quality. The author/creator may have deliberately lowered the quality of the propaganda to make it more acceptable to the TA.

The following five common terms are used when analyzing media selection:

1. **Frequency.** Frequency refers to how often a medium is disseminated. Newspapers or magazines may be daily, weekly, or monthly. Radio and TV may be daily, hourly, or weekly broadcasts. Social Media might be constant. Propaganda may appear multiple times across different mediums.

2. **Placement.** Placement is the physical location of author/creator's propaganda in a medium. In printed media, propaganda may be located in various parts of the paper. In audio and audiovisual mediums, propaganda can be located in a wide variety of places. On the internet it might appear in certain areas and not others. You may be able to evaluate the legitimacy of the propaganda by its placement in media.

3. **Place of Origin.** The place of origin is the production source of the propaganda. Examples are print plants, TV production studios, and broadcast stations, radio production studios and broadcast stations, advertising agencies, marketing firms, web development companies, websites,

social media accounts, and print media firms.

4. Technical Characteristics. Technical characteristics include such information as frequency, channel, modulation, signal strength, bandwidth, and other electronic signature means. TV propaganda characteristics include picture quality, sound quality, and color. Printed media may be classified by size and quality of paper, print colors, and print quality. Internet may be production quality classified by original video or picture production as opposed to re-used existing video clips or pictures. Sound quality is also a characteristic that should be noted.

5. Method of Dissemination. Method of dissemination is similar to dissemination source, as stated earlier in the source analysis.

EFFECTS

The most important, and often the most difficult, aspect of propaganda analysis to determine is its effectiveness on the ultimate TA. The ultimate measure of author/creator's propaganda effectiveness is the change in behavior or attitude of the TAs involved. Effects analysis is similar to determining the impact of the propaganda on its intended TAs; direct and indirect impact indicators are significant indicators of effectiveness. Impact indicators are events and observations that can eventually lead to a measured level of effectiveness. You may not always be able to gather actual impact indicators to evaluate the effects of an author/creator's propaganda and may have to evaluate its impact analytically.

General comments and input from the public through various means listed in the HUMINT chapter can be very helpful to your propaganda analysis. Look for Op-Eds, articles, podcasts, social media comments, comments in the comment sections of online local newspapers, etc. What follows is a portion of an analysis by Richard Williams Bulliet of Columbia University (NYC) about Osama bin Laden's recruitment video. The evaluation goes beyond effects and evaluates many other aspects of the video. Notice how his opinion provides valuable information regarding the effectiveness of the video and by using your OSINT skills you can further validate the source and his sentiment.

> *There is no way to calculate the effectiveness of this videotape. Some young Arab men who watch it find*

it gripping; some feel it contains nothing new.
Effective propaganda often contains nothing new,
however. It works by triggering latent feelings,
by manipulating familiar words and images.
Looked at strictly from a structural standpoint,
the bin Laden videotape shows a highly professional mind at work.
The psychological understanding of how propaganda can move
people to action is of a very high order, as are the technical skills
deployed in the video and sound editing. Though some propagandists
for the American side in the current conflict portray Osama bin Laden
as the enemy of America's modern technological civilization, this tape
proves that he is capable of using both the techniques and the
professional production skills of the modern television industry
to convey his message. Though never named in the tape or accorded
a rank or title confirming his implicit leadership, Osama bin Laden's face,
voice, and thinking dominate it throughout. Whoever the actual producer,
the animating intelligence is that of bin Laden, a man who shows himself
here as a master of propaganda and an intelligent, ruthless,
and, yes, modern adversary.

Richard Williams Bulliet | Columbia University (NYC)

If you want to create additional opportunities for analysis, you may

Chapter 8

decide to test the propaganda on the TAs by survey sampling, focus groups, or any of the other means of product pretesting and post testing. A drawback of this action is that you'll further be disseminating the propaganda. Another means of determining the effect of propaganda is to conduct surveys of the TAs involved. Evaluate the impact of propaganda on all applicable TAs—apparent, intermediate, unintended, and ultimate. This analysis may reveal errors or vulnerabilities for future exploitation. While conducting effects analysis, identify any linkages between the propaganda being analyzed and other known items of similar design. This step marks the beginning of a transition from individual propaganda analysis to potentially identifying an entire propaganda program, which would indicate a higher level of sophistication. Make sure to share your findings with friends and family to make them aware of what's really going on.

8-3   SCAME SAMPLE (U.S. Army Field Manual 3–05.302)

Source Analysis: What is the real source?   DTG: When last updated?
1. Elements of the source.
   a. Actor
   b. Author/Creator
   c. Authority

2. Type. White_____ Gray_____ Black_____
3. Credibility of each source element
     a. Actor
     b. Authority
     c. Author

Content Analysis: What does the propaganda say? What is it trying to get the TA to do?

1. Objective of the message.
2. Line of persuasion used.
3. Morale of the source.
4. Involuntary information in the message (news, opinions, and entertainment).
5. Biographical information (new leader, and so on)
6. Economic information.
7. Propaganda inconsistencies.
8. Intentions of agenda of the source.
9. Geographic information.

Audience Analysis: Who are the audiences?

1. Apparent audience.
     a. Perception of the message.

     b. Reason selected.
  2. Ultimate audience.
     a. Perception of the message.
     b. Reason selected.
  3. Intermediate audience.
     a. Perception of the message.
     b. Reason selected.
  4. Unintended audience.
     a. Perception of the message.
     b. Reason selected.

Media Analysis: What media are used and why?
  1. Type. Radio_____ Television_____ Print (specific type) _____
   Newspaper/Magazine_____ Internet_____ Other _____
  2. Frequency.
  3. Placement.
  4. Place of origin.
  5. Technical characteristics.
  6. Method of dissemination.
  7. Transmission mode.

Effects Analysis: What impact is this propaganda having?

Chapter 8

1. Methods used in analysis.
2. Impact indicators (direct and indirect).
3. Conclusions.

8-4   ANALYZE PROPAGANDA

OSINT can be used to identify and analyze propaganda, including visual and audio propaganda, by governments, intelligence agencies and a well-informed citizenry. This information can help better understand the motivations and goals of the organizations behind the propaganda, which can be useful in developing counter-propaganda strategies.

For example, the government or well-equipped citizenry of a country may use OSINT and the SCAME process to monitor and analyze propaganda spread by a foreign state to determine the motivations behind it and to develop a response. Another example could be a well-informed citizenry using OSINT to analyze propaganda spread by extremist organizations, to better understand their ideologies and tactics.

By gathering and analyzing information from multiple sources, the government and intelligence agencies can gain a comprehensive understanding of propaganda and its impact, which can help to inform their response.

One current example of the use of OSINT to identify and analyze propaganda is the tracking of disinformation campaigns related to elections. In recent years, there have been numerous instances of foreign actors using social media and other online platforms to spread false information and manipulate public opinion to interfere with the electoral process.

OSINT can be used to analyze the spread of this disinformation, to identify the sources behind it, and to assess its impact on a target audience. By using a combination of tools and techniques, including data mining, network analysis, and sentiment analysis, you'll be able to build a comprehensive understanding of the disinformation landscape targeted at the cognitive battlespace of your country. Use the tools you've been given and work as a team.

Chapter 8
Homework Break

Please consider all the information presented so far, while seeking additional information and using your critical thinking skills to answer these questions. Write your answers on this page.

1. How will Chapter 8 help you understand the real-life issues you learned about in Chapter 3?

2. According to section 8-2, what are the four major classifications of Target Audiences?

3. Based on section 8–2, explain in your own words why it is important to identify the type of source: (Actor, Authority, or Author/Creator?)

Chapter 9

AI Is the New Crack

I tried to kick ...
but that shit
be callin' me, man, it
be callin' me, man...
I just gotta go to it!

Pookie | New Jack City

9-1   FEEDING THE NEEDY

The CCP is the proverbial digital crack dealer. The Uniparty is the corrupt cop that protects the digital crack dealer, and you are a digital crackhead. Step away from the digital crack-pipe. What would happen if you changed your routine and limited the CCP's access to your mind? Do you really have to know every news update, all day long in every place in the world? Do you really have to know what your friends think about everything you do all day long? Do you really need to constantly interact with others who feed your "LIKE"-fetish? "Need" is the operative word.

9-2   THE FIRST STEP IS ADMITTING IT

If you aren't a business owner that uses social media to earn a living, if you aren't hopelessly bedridden, and if you aren't responsible for monitoring something internet based as part of your job *and* you're on the internet all day, well, then you're an addict. You have an addiction. Don't get mad: let's talk about it and come up with some solutions because it's not good for you or the children in your life.

9-3   GET YOUR GRIT TOGETHER

Creating a healthy balance between online and offline activities is not only essential for adults but also crucial for the well-being of children and grandchildren. By setting an example and teaching them responsible technology usage, we can equip them with the skills they need to navigate the digital world safely. Or we can allow them to stay addicted to dopamine, laziness, and digital manipulation. Creating a healthy balance between online and offline activities is essential in today's digital world. For example, after reading the news for an hour during breakfast, you could turn your phone off and stow it in a Faraday bag. Spend the morning engaged in an activity, such as jogging or attending a yoga class, or just be at work without giving your adversary access to your mind and constantly manipulating you.

Midday, retrieve your phone and respond to messages, enjoy lunch while scrolling through social media, and put the phone away after lunch, turned off and in a Faraday bag so it's not transmitting your location or listening to you. In the evening, check it again while waiting for dinner and then put it away. Use your time to participate in a local community event or spend quality time with family over dinner, board games, quality reading, or watching your favorite shows or movies on TV or other activities. Be human with humans. Too easy, right? Right!

9–4   COMPARTMENTALIZATION - TECH HYGIENE

Another option to better manage screen time, online addiction and exposure to AI-driven psychological programming is to consider using a dedicated tablet or smartphone solely for social media, news, and entertainment, and a separate smartphone for essential communication through encrypted texts and calls with a secure app. Don't forget your VPN, too. This will limit the manipulation from constantly coming through the phone you use to communicate with. Only use your tablet during designated "playtime". Think of it like recess you had in school. When not in use, store these devices in secure locations, such as locked drawers or safes, to reduce the risk of unauthorized access or data breaches.

9-5   BE A LEADER IN YOUR FAMILY – TECH DISCIPLINE

For families, implementing a dedicated entertainment device (computer, tablet, or smartphone) for all the kids to share will promote family interaction, foster healthy relationships, and enable parents and grandparents to monitor their children's and grandchildren's online exposure more effectively. Make your kids share one entertainment device between them at home for their online entertainment usage, and use parental controls to keep their individual phones stripped and blocked from downloading apps other than a secure encrypted text and phone app you've selected.

Establishing guidelines for the entertainment device usage, akin to setting curfews or chore schedules, will help strike a healthy balance between online and offline activities. When your children and grand-children are online, it's the equivalent of being out of your home and somewhere you don't know about, and the online manipulation seen in this Session II of *The Guide* shows you all the ways being online is more dangerous than being outside. The internet is a platform for psychological warfare, and you're giving our adversaries access to your children who are shaping them for the future. Shouldn't that be your job and not your adversary's?

9-6   HUMANS DO HUMAN THINGS

In the 1980s, the average 10-year-old had various ways to entertain themselves that often revolved around outdoor activities, and they fostered their imagination and social skills. Children would spend time outside riding bicycles with friends, exploring their neighbor-hoods, playing sports, making up outdoor games, and embarking on adventures. They also enjoyed playing with popular toys of the era, such as action figures, dolls, and building sets, engaging in hours of imaginative play. Board games and puzzles were a favorite pastime, with families and friends gathering around classics like Monopoly, Scrabble, and Sorry! Television and movies played a significant role in entertainment, as kids would watch popular cartoons and TV shows or enjoy films on VHS tapes. Nightly, families gathered in the living room to watch television together or they went to church. Lastly, outdoor games like tag, hide-and-seek, and kickball were common-place, with children frequently playing in their yards, local parks, or school playgrounds. Kids climbed trees, explored nearby woods, and all of these things are still options. They don't need to be on a device any different than kids needed to have 24-hour access to the home video-game console of the 80s. It's happening because you can't tear yourselves away, so you placate them with your drug of choice: digital crack.

A goal, a love, and a dream give you total control over your body and your life.
John Wayne | American Actor

9-7   THE CHEST POKE

Establishing these proposed guidelines ensures the younger generation has ample time for personal development, social skills, and education, but the vast majority of you won't make any of these changes. Right? Because as with all addictions, come excuses, denial, and deal making. You'll be unwilling to face potential loneliness and you won't change your comfort level. Not willingly. And why should you have to? The real problem is those who want to weaponize the things you enjoy. If we could unite to stop them, then we could have our cake and eat it too. Your legislators are doing a poor job of protecting you and your family from AI-driven psychological programming the same as they did a poor job of protecting people from pharma when they allowed the opioid epidemic or failed to stop the cocaine trade that led to neighborhood crack wars. It's time to make them do their jobs.

9–8   MAKE THE LEGISLATORS WORK

Push for domestic legislation that regulates AI systems, such as requiring AI-driven platforms to be transparent about their algorithms and data usage. Ensure that AI developers are held responsible for their creations by demanding legal accountability for AI carelessness, misuse, and abuse. Identify and remove the Uniparty members that stand in the way of this legislation. They are our biggest problem that prevents safe and sensible actions because they are corrupt and have been compromised.

9–9   ITEMS OF THE COMPREHENSIVE PLAN

Support initiatives that promote digital safety and literacy, such as educational programs in schools or community centers, to equip children and grandchildren with the knowledge and skills they need to protect themselves online from not just online predators but also AI-driven psychological programming. Encourage the younger generation to engage in local political events and become informed about digital safety and privacy issues, fostering a sense of civic responsibility. Doing this removes the most lethal weapon of our adversaries and the citizenry retains their rights.

9–10   NEUTER THE UNIPARTY AND FOREIGN INFLUENCE

Winning is doable so long as we have a viable plan and people are dedicated to executing the plan. It will take literally all of us, and we have to remember that most of the opposition messaging will be to falsely say the right to free speech is being threatened. But remember that the opposite is true because we are upholding the free people's speech and their way of life by denying access to manipulative foreign powers who are not protected by our laws that protect free speech. Free speech is for all of us who live in our country; free speech does not and should not protect foreign entities who are attempting to destroy freedom through AI-driven psychological programming. Remember these key items:

1. Any candidate running for public office and all supporting PACs should only be authorized to use registered AI systems, and they should be made available for public disclosure.

2. Support independent citizen journalism by subscribing to or sharing content from unbiased news sources and grassroots individuals, and/or media organizations.

3. Use your new OSINT and HUMINT skills to keep people honest (politicians, journalists, and friends) and to vet all critical news reports before sharing them. Use the Breaking-News Quarantine Rule ("72 Hours") to avoid IO Fratricide.

4. Use the SCAME process for suspected propaganda.

5. Accept the fact that you are human and act like one with other humans.

6. Be a leader in your family.

7. Don't think you can't be tricked. And know how they do it.

8. Engage in local political events to identify and remove Uniparty members who hinder the progress for digital safety and privacy for the citizenry.

9. Build the Coalition of Governors and make your state self-sufficient. The Coalition of Governors must be formed immediately with the commitment of making their states more independent of the federal government by developing sustainably sourced in-state programs to ensure access to food, energy, and water. Expect the federal government to fall, and focus on your state, now. You have the control.

10. Demand legislative requirements based on principles listed in section 5-5 of this Session II.

You can enjoy a safer and more fulfilling online experience while minimizing the risks of manipulation, misinformation, and privacy breaches.

Chapter 9

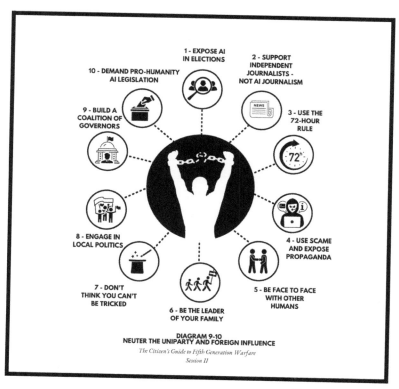

DIAGRAM 9-10
NEUTER THE UNIPARTY AND FOREIGN INFLUENCE

The Citizen's Guide to Fifth Generation Warfare
Session II

MAKE IT HAPPEN

By taking these steps, we can ensure a safer and more fulfilling online experience for our children and grandchildren, minimizing the risks of manipulation, misinformation, and privacy breaches while promoting critical thinking and responsible digital behavior. This not only benefits the younger generation by taking the digital crackpipe out of their mouths, but it also contributes to our national security, strengthens families, and fosters a well-informed society.

Be prepared to change your own mind, because as you use the techniques for defeating AI manipulation, you may find that you're one of the many that was taken advantage of. You may come to see that what you've believed in the past was not the truth, and that's okay. Expect your worldview to change, and let good data and good technique be what helps you know what the truth is so you can put your polarization where it truly belongs.

Your neighbor is not your enemy. We must get beyond the years of our personal and institutionalized cognitive dissonance if we're sincere about fighting AI and ending the AI-driven psychological pro-gramming that's killing us. The simple truth is that if it makes sense to defend the physical space of a country with physical borders to deter our enemies, then it makes sense to protect the cognitive space of the people who live within the borders of a country with a digital border (mega firewall) to protect them from foreign-born AI-driven psychological programming.

Now you know about one of your adversary's main centers of gravity, and you've been given the tools you need to disrupt and dismantle it. Be bold, spread this message, and make the changes happen. You know how your adversary behaves, and you have the comprehensive strategy to protect your family and defend your country. You have new tools to determine what the truth is and you have each other. If you want to fight the effects of AI that are destroying your family, your country, and your future, you can!

See this QR code for proposed legislation that you can support and ask your legislators to support it. Send it to them and demand they take action. If they don't use it, ask them why and demand to know what their solutions are.

Chapter 9
Homework Break

Please consider all the information presented so far, while seeking additional information and using your critical thinking skills to answer these questions. Write your answers on this page.

1. After reading Session II, list five reasons why legislation is needed.

2. Compare and contrast tech hygiene and tech discipline.

3. Does the U.S. Constitution protect speech coming from a foreign power or does it protect free speech of American and legal residents in America?

4. In the modern world, why are digital borders just as important as physical borders?

5. Are you represented best by the John Wayne quote or the Pookie quote?

6. When will you answer all the Homework Questions? Do it as a group with friends

Chapter 9

ADMIN NOTE

Keep Session II with you for a reference guide to answer your questions as you see the things you've learned present themselves. Explain what you've learned to others and have good conversations. This is more than a red pill: it's a silver bullet. But it's also a lot to remember, so keep it on-hand.

Appendix 1

Michael T. Flynn, LTG, U.S. Army, (Retired)
BIOGRAPHY WITH COMMENTARY

LT. GENERAL MICHAEL T. FLYNN served over thirty-three years of service in the United States military, which culminated in his position as the Director of the Defense Intelligence Agency (DIA) and the nation's highest serving military intelligence officer.

Flynn dared to oppose former President Obama's false narrative about ISIS as a "JV team" when Islamic extremist groups around the world were growing in number and strength, posing an increasingly dangerous risk, as seen later when radical Islamist terrorist group attacks escalated. Not only did Flynn oppose Obama when testifying to a congressional committee in 2014 (and was subsequently fired), but Flynn also wrote a national-selling book about Obama's negligence, which was published in 2016. And then he had the audacity to campaign for President Donald J. Trump.

Appendix 1: Biography with Commentary by Lt. General (Ret.) Michael T. Flynn

Destroying Flynn's impeccable reputation was like a "twofer" for Obama, who was also aiming for someone even higher on his list: President Donald J. Trump. Fifteen days prior to President Trump's inauguration, President Obama, then-Vice President Biden, then-FBI Director James Comey, and other senior government officials

gathered in the Oval Office on January 5, 2017, to conspire and cover up their treasonous spying on the Trump campaign and presidency while plotting retribution against Flynn. This was an attempt to derail Trump's presidency before it even had a chance to begin. Subsequently, a weaponized Department of Justice (DOJ) attempted to entrap Flynn, but ultimately the case was withdrawn by the DOJ stating there was no crime committed, an egregious demonstration and statement of corruption by the DOJ. However, getting out of the corrupt clutches of the Judge who presided over his case, President Trump issued Flynn a pardon of innocence. At the time of the January 5th meeting in the Oval Office, Flynn was the incoming National Security Advisor and previous Director of the Defense Intelligence Agency and would have thwarted the efforts to undermine the Trump presidency. Flynn was an important key player to the America First movement and President Trump because of his background, knowledge, and determination to expose globalist actions that were not in America's best interests.

Flynn has authored two books: the national bestseller, *The Field of Fight* and *A Letter to America: The Time to Fight for Your Faith And Family Is NOW.* You can

Appendix 1: Biography with Commentary by Lt. General (Ret.) Michael T. Flynn

learn more about General Flynn at his website: www.generalflynn.com

WHY I DECIDED TO CO-WRITE THIS GUIDE

First, I was honored and privileged to serve in the United States Army for over 33 years and to have gotten to know and work alongside some of the bravest, smartest, and most courageous patriots on the planet. One of those patriots is my co-author, Sergeant Boone Cutler, an amazing and gifted soldier. If you have never met a true American patriot, go speak to a soldier in the United States Army. They will renew your faith in everything you believe is good and right. I served in conventional and special operations units as well as in several training commands focusing primarily on intelligence, security, operations, and counter-intelligence issues among many other "art of war" disciplines.

I learned an awful lot serving in the Army, but I principally learned more about myself than anything else. As I travel around the country these days, interacting with thousands of grassroots Americans, I find myself explaining to people things I learned during my military training, things about warfare that I take as second nature. From these many interactions, both the questions and my responses, I felt strongly that creating some type of *Citizen's Guide* for the type of war we're facing here at home was not only necessary, but vital.

Those of us who serve in various parts of our government take an oath to support

Appendix 1: Biography with Commentary by Lt. General (Ret.) Michael T. Flynn

and defend our constitution against all enemies, foreign and domestic. In my decades of experiences overseas preparing and training and then fighting to defend our country from foreign adversaries, I never dreamed the greatest battles to be waged would be right here in our homeland against subversive elements of our own government. That said, Boone Cutler and I decided to capture significant and important lessons and skills each of us developed in our time serving our country and share them with freedom-loving people across America and the world over.

I pray this *Guide* allows readers to gain a vastly better appreciation of the different generations of warfare that exist and how the fifth generation of war (5GW) is now impacting our daily lives. Our nation is a constitutional republic where consent of the governed is paramount. We remain a beautiful experiment in democracy, but like our founders envisioned, it can only be maintained by an engaged citizenry. Our families, our neighbors and communities, and our nation and the freedom of humanity globally, deserve our active participation. For without it, we will succumb to tyranny, and like many nations throughout history, we will no longer exist. The authors strongly believe that citizens can engage far better when they are better informed. That is why at this epic moment in history, I felt *The Citizen's Guide to Fifth Generation Warfare* was required.

GF

Appendix 1: Biography with Commentary by Lt. General (Ret.) Michael T. Flynn

Appendix 2

Boone Cutler, SGT, U.S. Army, (Retired)
BIOGRAPHY WITH COMMENTARY

BOONE CUTLER served as the Psychological Operations team sergeant in the war with Iraq whose team was responsible for Sadr City (2005-2006). Following the war, he released *CallSign Voodoo,* which was written in real-time from the Warfighter's perspective while deployed to Iraq in Sadr City and during his subsequent two-year hospitalization at Walter Reed Army Medical Center for injuries sustained during combat operations.

Cutler's book, *FPL: Boone Cutler Protocols for Warfighters,* was written about overcoming his prescription drug addictions, fighting with suicide, dealing with PTSD and Traumatic Brain Injury, and pursuing the alternative medical treatments that worked for him and currently work for other Warfighters.

Cutler is the former radio talk show host of "Tipping Point with Boone Cutler:

Appendix 2: Biography with Commentary by Boone Cutler

The Warfighter Perspective." He spends his time promoting the veteran and first responder anti-suicide campaign "Spartan Pledge" which is based on the warrior ethos. You can learn more about Boone Cutler at his website: www.boonecutler. com.

WHY I DECIDED TO CO-WRITE THIS GUIDE

I think it's important to get a few things in the open. For one reason, I'm 100% sure the release of this *Guide* will put me on the shitlist of some powerful people who have a lot of powerful friends. The techniques described in *The Citizen's Guide to Fifth Generation Warfare* can easily be turned on me and my family. I expect they will. The decision to co-write this *Guide* came with all my family in mind. I'm sure the rumors surrounding this project will be amazing – I can't wait to watch how it plays out.

Here's the TOP 10 rumors I anticipate:

1. General Flynn and some psychological operations guy are secretly building a militia.
2. Boone is related to the Rothschilds, and he's in the CIA.
3. His other books are satanic, and he's really a Russian woman.
4. Boone Cutler is a white supremacist who was part of a racist motorcycle gang.

Appendix 2: Biography with Commentary by Boone Cutler

5. The photos of Boone Cutler in Sadr City are photoshopped; he never served.
6. Boone Cutler is a plant from the Rockefeller family.
7. His tattoos have secret meanings about Adrenochrome.
8. He's the PSYOP guy working behind the scenes with General Flynn to create QAnon.
9. He worked at George Magazine with JFK Jr., and he is an FBI informant.
10. Boone is a misogynist who hates gays, transexuals, and chinchillas.

Watch it happen. You'll know they are most desperate when they attack my family with emotional-based messaging. We're ready. Halfhearted jokes aside, a few years ago some friends and I (retired Special Operations guys from the Army, Navy and Marine Corps, and former old-school CIA folk) were discussing things happening in America and the world when the smart-ass question came up, "Hey bro, does this shit look familiar?" The resounding response among us all was, "Yup!". Later, when a lot of us were helping get our allies out of Afghanistan after the botched withdrawal, Special Operations folk from other countries joined the group, too, from the U.K., Australia, Canada, etc. We are everywhere.

After the main effort was over in Afghanistan, a chunk of us were like . . . okay, what's next? We were pissed off. We're very smart and superbly trained, and we've seen our fair share of combat. Military veterans love being with each other, and we're

Appendix 2: Biography with Commentary by Boone Cutler

loyal to each other because of it. The idea for *The Citizen's Guide to Fifth Generation Warfare* was spawned at that time. Though few know it, we all specialize in non-kinetic (non-violent) warfare, and we're some of the guys who shape environments (political, social, economic) in foreign countries on behalf of our country.

People know what artillery is and what it does, but they don't know anything about 5GW. If we were being attacked with artillery, the proper response would be for an engineer and an artilleryman to train the citizenry how to survive an artillery attack. The challenge here is teaching people what Fifth Generation Warfare (5GW) attacks are and what to do about them. The best people to train the citizenry about the non-kinetic aspects of the irregular war that's happening now come from the Intelligence and Special Operations communities. Ultimately, this *Citizen's Guide* is part of an information campaign that exposes Fifth Generation Warfare.

I contributed to this *Guide* because the method of attack against humanity is my wheelhouse. I'm a boots-on-the-ground guy. Developing PSYOP campaigns and working face-to-face with target audiences has been my game. General Flynn and I are a great mash up because his game is Intel from the highest levels, and the dude has mad smarts. He's also been the target of shadowy government people and groups who used tactics written in this guide against him. He's been a true American, a great partner for this project, and a wealth of first-hand knowledge. If you knew what I know, you'd have an amazing

Appendix 2: Biography with Commentary by Boone Cutler

level of respect for the fight he's been through.

It's my duty to protect my family, my country, and humanity from destruction. Whoever attacks me or General Flynn after the release of this guide is looking to protect and promote the destruction we seek to stop. They can all eat a bag of glass. We will not relent, and attacks against us will only strengthen the resolve of the people who've read the guide and the communities of people who know the information it contains. At this point, attacking us is the same as promoting us. They don't have the resources to win unless they go "full-Stalin" and start whacking people indiscriminately. Even then, it would only accelerate the victory for freedom-loving people everywhere.

The way we win in 5GW starts by educating the citizenry about the war they are a part of in the cognitive terrain that is being conducted by the UniParty, state actors, and non-state actors. Only then can people freely make logical decisions for themselves. That's the goal here. The flies will soon be free from the flypaper.

Now you know my story. Get to work! Thanks for reading. And truthfully, I do hate chinchillas, but the other TOP 10 rumors are bullshit.

All the way! | Boone

Thank you for reading SESSION I

Appendix 2: Biography with Commentary by Boone Cutler

Other Books by
LTG Michael T. Flynn and Boone Cutler

Session 2: How To Fight Artificial Intelligence (AI): THE CITIZEN'S GUIDE TO FIFTH GENERATION WARFARE by Michael T. Flynn and Boone Cutler

How to Fight Artificial Intelligence (AI) unmasks the realm of AI-driven psychological programming and a strategy to combat Ai's invisible manipulative power.

The Field of Fight: How We Can Win the Global War Against Radical Islam and Its Allies by Lieutenant General (Ret.) Michael T. Flynn and Michael Ledeen

The Field of Fight succinctly lays out why we have failed to stop terrorist groups from growing. The core message is that if you understand your enemies, it's a lot easier to defeat them.

Summary of The Field of Fight by Michael T. Flynn with Michael Ledeen, Kindle Edition.

The Summary of The Field of Fight by Michael T. Flynn with Michael Ledeen includes an analysis.

A Letter to America: The Time to Fight for Your Family is NOW by General Michael T. Flynn. What can you do when vicious enemies assault all that is good? When the destiny of the United States is at stake, the future of the entire world is threatened. Achieving our destiny as a freedom-loving nation, Providence compels us to do our part in our communities. God bless America. Let's stand by everything that was and is good in our lives, in our communities, and in our country.

Other Books by LTG Michael T. Flynn and Boone Cutler

CallSign Voodoo : A Firsthand Account of How One PsyOp'er and His Team Conducted a Battle of Wits with the Mehdi Militia in Sadr City, Iraq by Boone Cutler.

In 2005, a four-man PsyOp team was assigned to Sadr City, a violent Baghdad neighborhood of more than 2.5 million. *The mission?* Turn the ideological tide against insurgent leader Muqtada Al Sadr and his Mehdi militia. *The means?* Psychological operations: non-kinetic force. Written in boots-on-the-ground-real time, Boone unveils the power of psychological warfare against learned helplessness.

FPL: Boone Cutler Protocols for Warfighters by Boone Cutler and Geoff Dardia

FPL stands for "Functional Personal Lifestyle" which is a collection of health & wellness protocols put together by Warfighters Boone Cutler and Geoff Dardia for Warfighters (combat veterans) who have made the decision to take their healing into their own hands.

Other Books by LTG Michael T. Flynn and Boone Cutler

Printed in the USA
CPSIA information can be obtained
at www.ICGtesting.com
LVHW061524190424
777774LV00020B/399

9 781088 216231